P9-BIF-817

THE
UPSTAIRS
ROOM

Also by Johanna Reiss

THE JOURNEY BACK

Johanna Reiss

THE UPSTAIRS ROOM

HarperTrophy®

A Division of HarperCollins*Publishers*

Harper Trophy® is a registered trademark
of HarperCollins Publishers Inc.

The Upstairs Room
Copyright © 1972 by Johanna Reiss
All rights reserved. No part of this book may be used or
reproduced in any manner whatsoever without written permission
except in the case of brief quotations embodied in critical
articles and reviews. Printed in the United States of America.
For information address HarperCollins Children's Books, a division
of HarperCollins Publishers, 10 East 53rd Street, New York, NY 10022.
ISBN 0-690-85127-8.—ISBN 0-690-04702-9 (lib. bdg.)
Library of Congress Catalog Card Number 77-187940
ISBN 0-06-440370-X (pbk.)
Published in hardcover by HarperCollins Publishers.
First Harper Trophy edition, 1990.
10 11 12 13   LP/CW   30 29 28

THIS BOOK is about my life, or rather part of my life, the part that took place in Holland during the Second World War. In this book I have gone back to those years, when I was a child, and Jewish, and therefore undesirable, when I had to hide from the Germans.

I have not tried to write a historical book, although it may have some historical value. What I *did* try to write was a simple, human book, in which my sister and I suffered and complained, and sometimes found fault with the Gentile family that took us in for a few years, in which the members of that family were not heroes but people, with strengths and weaknesses.

JOHANNA REISS

For the memory of Jim

INTRODUCTION

THE Second World War started in 1939 when the German army marched into Poland, but the war had been in the making for many years, perhaps twenty, ever since the Germans lost the First World War and were forced to sign a peace settlement that they considered unreasonably harsh and humiliating. They especially resented the fact that they were not allowed more than a token army. Many veterans could not find jobs and looked angrily for an outlet for their energies.

Adolf Hitler had been an impassioned soldier in the German army during the First World War, and he was even more upset than most when Germany lost the war. He decided to go into politics and bring back glory to his country. He had an incredible hatred of Jews, and he blamed them for Germany's defeat; he blamed others, too. Not the German soldiers though. They had been brave, he said, and capable, and would never have lost the war. Many discontented Germans

—among them the dissatisfied war veterans—whole-heartedly agreed with Hitler's ideas and joined his budding Nazi party. They were convinced that under his leadership Germany's humiliation and defeat would be wiped out. He had said they would be.

In 1933, after Hitler became chancellor of Germany, the Nazi party was designated the only legal one. He started to rebuild the army, something the peace settlement did not permit him to do, but the world was trying to recover from a severe economic depression, and was too busy with problems of its own to stop Hitler. Most Germans wanted Germany to be a strong military country and were delighted with his actions. Schools taught students how wonderful military power was and that, according to Hitler and the millions of devoted members of the Nazi party, Jews were responsible for almost all the evil things in the world and should be punished. The German radio, newspapers, and movies told the public the same things. Hatred of Jews spread, and soon official decisions were made to fire Jews from their jobs, to take away their property, to beat them, and eventually to kill them.

Hitler's plans to establish Germany as the dominant world power were already well underway when on the first of September, 1939, his army invaded Poland. Two days later England and France declared war on Germany, and almost immediately these two allied nations were joined by others, including Canada and Australia. Far from discouraged, the Germans plowed through much of northwestern Europe in the spring and early summer of 1940. Denmark was the first country they took, followed by Norway, Holland, Belgium, Luxembourg, and France. In every country they occupied, the Germans established an efficient machinery for the punishment of Jews.

In April 1941, Hitler's soldiers attacked in North Africa, to help Germany's partner Italy in the battle against British power there, and in June 1941, the Germans marched into Russia. Hitler was delirious with success. Before his troops entered Russia, though, Hitler had made a promise to Japan. He would stand by that nation in case of a clash between Japan and the United States. The clash came in December 1941, and Hitler declared war on America, only a few hours before the United States itself declared war on Germany and Italy.

Hitler had no idea how great Russia and America's strength would be. For the next three and a half years many battles were fought, and little by little the German soldiers had to leave every country they had occupied. Even her own land became a battleground, and in the spring of 1945, the Russians and the Allies met in Berlin. The war was over.

It had been horrible. People all over the world had suffered. This story tells of the sufferings of Jews in Holland.

1

I WAS not very old in 1938, just six, and a little thing. Little enough to fit between the wall and Father's chair, which in those days was always pulled up in front of the radio. He sat with his face close to the radio, bent forward, with his legs spread apart, his arms resting on his knees. And he listened.

"Father, look at this." I held out a drawing I had made.

"Ssht."

"Father, I asked you to. . . ."

He listened, but not to me.

Where was Austria, which Hitler had attached to Germany in the spring? It was not a nice thing to have done, I guessed. Father had looked angry.

Hitler. All the man on the radio ever talked about was Hitler. He must be an important man in Germany. Why didn't he like German Jews? Because he didn't. Why else would he be bothering them. The radio said he did.

"Father . . ."

"Ssht."

Or why would he let Jews buy food only at certain hours? Or arrest them and put them in jail? Only the jail was called a camp. But Germany wasn't Holland. I smiled. A good thing! If we lived in Germany, Hitler might do the same thing to us. He must have been the man who had just told the German people they could steal things from Jews. Anything they liked they could take. Or burn. The German people could even arrest Jews, just like that.

The radio said something had happened. A Jewish boy had killed a German man. That wasn't nice. But allowing people to run through the streets in Germany one night and do all those things to the Jews was not nice either. It had a special name that night: *Kristallnacht*.

"Father, what does *Kristallnacht* mean?"

"Ssht, Annie. I'm listening."

That was all Father said to me these days. And I didn't like it. He used to say much more to me, nice things. Even play with me. How could I ever find out anything if he never answered questions? I got to my feet. Mother would tell me. I walked into her bedroom to ask her what the word *Kristallnacht* meant, but she had a headache again. How come bad kidneys give you headaches?

Well anyway, Germany wasn't Holland. I frowned. Winterswijk was near the German border though, less than twenty minutes away. That's how close it was.

Some farmers lived so close to the border that their cows grazed in Germany, only across the road from their houses. I knew because Father was a cattle dealer, and he often took me with him when he went to buy cows.

I was glad we lived right in Winterswijk, not so close to Germany that you could see it from your room. I saw something much nicer when I looked out of my window: the house of the Gans family, which was right across the street. The Ganses often waved to me at night when I leaned out the window—the old man and woman and their big son. "Get back in bed," they'd call, "or we'll tell your mother."

That wouldn't be bad. As long as they didn't tell my sisters. I had two of them, Sini and Rachel. Big sisters, sixteen and twenty-one. And then there was Marie, our sleep-in maid, who was almost like a sister. We all lived in our house in the center of town, away from that border.

After the bad night in Germany, a meeting was held at our house. The Gans family came, all three of them, and Uncle Bram, who was in the cattle business with Father, and his wife. Uncle Phil was there without his wife because Aunt Billa and Mother didn't speak to each other. It had to do with my grandmother, who lived with Aunt Billa and Uncle Phil but who came to our house every day to complain about them. I knew. I had heard her. When I sat at the top of the stairs, I could hear a great deal, whether the voices came from

3

the bedroom upstairs or from the living room downstairs, as they did now. They were excited voices: "We
must help those German Jews who cross the border to
come to Winterswijk. . . . They left everything behind
in Germany. . . ." "They need our help. I talked to
some today. . . ." "Big raw scar on the face of one. . .
German soldier . . . with whip."

"But why?" That was Mother.

"Because he was a Jew, Sophie." Father sounded
impatient.

"It can't happen here . . . safe here . . . this isn't
Germany . . . this is Holland, you know. . . ." "That
Hitler has war on his mind, Sophie, . . . and we're
Jews, too. . . ."

There, footsteps. I ran back to my room and climbed
in bed. I pulled the blankets over my head.

A few months later Uncle Bram and his wife left for
America. We went to the station to say good-bye. They
must have been planning to stay for a long time. They
took a lot of suitcases with them. And it must be far
away, for Uncle Bram said that Hitler would never be
able to reach them in America.

"Sophie, why don't we go too?" Father said.

But Mother said she had too many headaches to
leave Holland and start all over again. Waving, we
remained at the station until the train went. With
angry steps Father walked over to his car, opened it,
and got in. He slammed the door and drove away,
leaving us to walk home.

4

By the fall of 1939, Rachel had graduated from teachers' college. She found a job at one of the nursery schools in Winterswijk. Sini started to work on a farm. At night when Father and Mother went across the street to sit outside with the Gans family, Mother tried to talk about my sisters. "That Rachel . . . so capable . . . and Sini, studying for her milking diploma. . . ." But I could tell from my window that nobody was listening to her. They were talking about the Germans who had invaded Poland.

That was a bad thing to have done, Rachel told me. So bad that England and France had said to Germany, "Get your soldiers out of Poland, or else." But Hitler had just laughed, and now England and France were at war with Germany. Served him right.

Why did I have to go to bed so early? It was still light out. After all, I was in second grade now. Tomorrow I would refuse to do it. I stuck my head farther out the window. Nobody looked up to tell me that I had to go back to bed, not even Mrs. Gans. They were too busy talking.

That winter the Gans family spent almost every night at our house, in front of the radio. They didn't have one of their own. Hitler did not seem to like Polish Jews either. He seemed to like them even less than German Jews. He had had some of them beaten so hard they had died, and they hadn't even done anything. How did he dare? I was often glad when Mother told me that it was time for me to go to bed. Under the blankets I couldn't hear the radio.

5

"Sophie," Father said, "we can't stay here any longer. We *must* go to America. I just heard that the German army is in Denmark and Norway. Sophie, that's close! Do you hear me? We have no choice. We're Jews!"

"Ies, you know I don't feel well. How can I leave? You're shouting so my head hurts even more. Annie, go to the kitchen and play there."

Unwillingly I left. Why did Mother always have to have headaches?

Father started to build a house outside of Winterswijk, where Mother felt we would be about as safe as in America. It made Father furious to hear her say that. But he built the house anyway. The house wasn't going to be near that border. No, it would be far away, on the other side of Winterswijk. The Germans would not bother us there.

And then it was May 10, 1940. In the middle of the night I woke up. So much noise. I jumped out of bed. Where was everybody? They were on their way downstairs. I ran downstairs, too.

"What's happening?" I asked. "I hear planes. What are they going to do?"

"I'm sure they're German planes," Rachel said.

"Maybe there's war here, too," Sini said.

"This is it," Father mumbled. "Now it's our turn."

"How do you know they're German planes?" Mother asked.

"They're coming from the east. Can't you hear?" Father snapped.

The border was to the east. Why wasn't the new

house ready? We'd be safe there. Mother had said so.

Father turned on the radio. The doorbell rang, and the Gans family stormed in. "What does the radio say?" "War, isn't it? We knew it." "What, the Germans are also in Belgium and Luxembourg?"

"Sophie, what are you doing?" Father asked.

Mother was taking silver from a drawer. "We have to hide it," she said. "They'll come and take it from us."

"Goddammit, stuff it back in the drawer."

"I'm going to bed," Rachel said, "and I'll stay in bed till the war's over."

"How long will that be?" I asked.

"Can't last more than a few days," Rachel answered.

Father laughed. But his face scared me.

When it was light and the noise had stopped, we went outside. Our house was a few blocks away from the marketplace, the real center of town. Rachel held my hand tightly. She hadn't gone to bed. We met several people who looked just as bewildered as we did. At the marketplace we stopped. German tanks were there, and German soldiers. In the same area where twice a week flowers were sold—tulips in the spring, roses in the summer.

Shivering, we leaned against the church wall. Grandmother, Uncle Phil, Aunt Billa, and my cousin Hannie were there, too. We looked at each other, but said nothing.

Several men were handing out cigars to the soldiers and slapping them on their shoulders.

"**Why are they** doing that?" I asked Rachel.

"They're Nazis," she whispered, "people who think like Hitler. NSB-ers we call them in Holland."

One of them walked over to Mrs. Gans. "Aren't they nice boys?" he asked. "Don't look so scared. They won't do a thing to you." He turned around and winked at one of the soldiers.

The soldier asked him something. "The shortest route to Enschede?" the NSB-er repeated. "First road to your left. That'll get you there. Hurry up. Here, take another cigar for the road." He closed the box. It was empty. On his way past us, he spat at our feet.

As we walked home, I asked Rachel why he had done that—spat at us. Because we were Jews, she said. But he wasn't German, and how did he know we were Jews? I asked. We looked different, she answered, darker. Rachel knew so much. No wonder she was a teacher. When I got home, I was going to see how different I looked.

Hitler did it again. He must have a great many soldiers, for now they were all over France, too. But nothing had happened to us that summer: no stealing, no beatings, nothing. Maybe Hitler liked Dutch Jews better than he did the others.

On clear nights Father sat with the Gans family again. "Jews here won't be bothered," the Gans son said, "not in this country."

I liked what he said. But Hitler must have changed his mind about liking Dutch Jews because in September Father was no longer allowed to do business. He read about it on a big poster that was stuck on a tree in the middle of the marketplace. He didn't care, he said, and went to the farmers anyway, but not to all his customers. He only went to those who liked Jews, and who wouldn't tell the Germans that Father still came to them to buy and sell cows. He got into the habit of stopping every day at that tree to see whether there were new notices. I wished the house was ready. Building it was taking an awfully long time.

Early in October, Marie came into the living room, closed the door, and stood against it. "Mrs. de Leeuw," she said nervously, "I have to tell you something."

"Yes?"

"I'm so miserable because of it. If you knew how I felt."

"What is it?" Mother asked in a worried voice.

"You've always been good to me, and I like the girls very much, and I hate to do it. But, see, it's my boyfriend."

"What about him?"

"He's afraid. He wants me to leave you."

"Why?"

"See, he says I might get in trouble if I keep working for you."

"What kind of trouble, Marie?"

"You see, because you're Jewish. And I don't mind, and he doesn't mind. We like Jews, but he's afraid a lot of people won't talk to me anymore if I stay with you. You understand?"

"I do," Mother said slowly.

I didn't. Why was she leaving? There had been nothing about it on that tree. Sini had to stay home and help Mother. It made her cry, Sini.

The next month Rachel received a letter in the mail. It was written in German, but she could read it anyway. After she had, she started running up and down the living room.

"Stop. You're making me dizzy," Mother complained. "And what are you doing anyway?"

"I've been fired," Rachel answered. "As of tomorrow."

"Annie, go out and play," Mother said.

I got as far as the door.

"But I'm not taking it," Rachel cried. "This letter came from the Germans, not from the school. The school probably doesn't even know about it. I'm going to the principal's house right now to get it straightened out."

"What a situation," Mother mumbled as Rachel stormed out of the house.

Rachel had been right. The principal hadn't known anything about the letter. He was upset, and sorry. But he said it would be better if Rachel didn't come back anymore. After all, that's what the letter said.

I had my own problems at school. Willy Bos, my best friend, didn't sit next to me any longer. Her mother had come to school to talk to the teacher. When she left, the teacher told me to sit somewhere else. By myself. Because I talked too much. But Willy said later that she wasn't allowed to sit next to me anymore because I was Jewish. Why was I Jewish anyway?

"Don't cry," Mother said to me, "we like you."

I knew that. But why didn't Willy? Anymore.

Father was angry about Willy. He knew her father very well. Dr. Bos was a vet and had taken care of Father's cattle for years.

"Sophie," Father said, "the longer we stay in Holland, the more intolerable life's going to be for us. This time, and I don't care what you say, I'm going to write to Bram. I'm going to ask him to help us get out of here, fast. If it isn't too late already."

How could we leave, Mother argued, when the new house wasn't even ready?

Father didn't listen. He was already writing the letter.

But it was too late. Uncle Bram couldn't help us get to America. And nobody in Holland would give Father the papers he needed, either.

In the spring of 1941, the tree began to have many announcements on it. We couldn't rent rooms anymore in hotels. With Mother sick almost all the time now, we wouldn't have done that anyway. But why did the next poster say that Jews could no longer go to beaches and parks? That wasn't fair. Beaches and parks belonged to everybody! The tree didn't mention woods, though, and Winterswijk had pretty ones. And so many.

11

The first announcements had made Father angry, but not nearly as angry as the one which said that everybody had to register at the town hall. "Everybody," he yelled. "Only the papers *we* have to carry with us have something extra on them! A big *J. J* for Jew! Sophie, what have you got to say now? Bram was smart. Boy, was he smart! And so was his wife."

"But, Ies, I never kept you from going," Mother said. "You could have gone yourself. With the children even. I would have managed."

"Oh, sure." Father laughed.

I looked at his face. How come I was never scared before when he laughed? I slammed the door as I went outside, just as Father had done a second before me.

Sometimes the tree talked to everyone. When food was going to be rationed, it did. We had expected the rationing, and had a lot of dried beans and cans of food in the cellar.

"What would you like," I asked Willy Bos. "Peas?" I answered. "I'm sorry but I don't have any. Maybe I'll get them in again. Maybe. Why don't you buy beans, Willy?" I held out a can. "Here, take it. They're good. You used to like them. Remember?"

Disgustedly I put down the can. Playing with an imaginary friend was no fun. I didn't like this summer vacation.

When school started again, I was in the fourth grade, but only for a few weeks: Jewish children were no longer allowed to attend school. I read the announcement at the marketplace and ran home. "I'm very glad," I said. "I hope I never have to go back."

But really it was boring not to go to school. Everybody else went. My cousin Hannie didn't go either, but I didn't like to visit her. Aunt Billa always made me wash my hands, even when there was nothing wrong with them. Poor Grandmother, having to live with her. No wonder she complained.

The vacation was a short one. In a couple of rooms near the synagogue a school was started for all the Jewish children from around Winterswijk.

"There'll be two men teachers," Father said, "and you're to pay attention."

I nodded. Sure I would. Maybe somebody would sit next to me again like before. Before I became Jewish.

Sini took me a few times to the new school, and then I wanted to go by myself. What was the matter with my teacher, I wondered. He praised everything I did. I wished he'd stop. The other children stuck their tongues out at me. Every afternoon he asked me to stay for a minute. "Take this note to Sini and don't lose it. I know I can depend on you. Right? Such a smart girl. And, eh, say hello to her."

Sini's face would get red when she read Mr. Herschel's note. "You give him this note tomorrow. Okay? But don't you open it."

What was the matter with both of them? I should ask Rachel. She'd know.

On my way to school I had started to notice signs saying *Joden verboden* ("forbidden to Jews"). The signs were on the walls of several restaurants and at the movie theater. I never went to the movies anyway. Mother wouldn't even let me go when Mickey Mouse was playing and everybody I knew went. "It would be too exciting for her," she always said.

It was a pity about the restaurants. We used to go sometimes. Until those signs.

But the other thing was worse. One day after school, a group of children from the old school was waiting for us. We kept on walking as if nothing was the matter, talking to each other as if we hadn't noticed them. Until they started chasing us. Lots of them, all yelling:

> "Jew, Jew, ugly mole,
> Stick your face in a dirty hole.
> Stick your face in a mustard pot,
> By tomorrow Jew will rot!"

How could we pretend nothing was the matter? We were running, weren't we? The others were chasing us, weren't they? When they caught up with us, they sang that song right in our ears. And hit. And kicked. To be chased by Willy Bos! I didn't like her either, not anymore. Why weren't we living in the new house yet?

I told them at home about being chased. "Don't worry," Sini said, "from now on I'll pick you up."

And then the new house was almost ready.

"I don't want to wait any longer," Father said. "I'm becoming very nervous about staying in town. We're moving."

"But, Ies," Mother complained, "we can't move into a house that hasn't been painted."

"Yes, we can," Father said. "If you don't want to come, I'm going by myself." He picked up the telephone and talked to somebody about the move.

Two days later an empty van pulled up in front of our old house. Father and a man carried the furniture out, the man careful at first, until he saw that Father threw everything on the van. Mother sat on a kitchen chair, turning her head back and forth, following the men with the furniture. She stayed there until they needed her chair to put on the van.

The Gans family waved as we left, all three of them.

It was almost October 1941.

2

The new house stood all by itself in the middle of meadows and fields. In the distance—but not too far away—I could see the top part of the church, the one in the marketplace at Winterswijk. Father brought home a little brown dog for me—Bobbie. When he gave it to me, he picked me up and hugged me, just as if there was no war. In the afternoons, after school, Bobbie and I went for walks. Instead of people, we met cows, and they were always eating. Did they keep their eyes open when they ate? I bent down to study one of them. She didn't even notice me. She was too busy with the grass.

I stood in the field for a long time. It was getting chilly. What time was it? Weren't they getting worried at home? They used to in the old house. Once they even called the police when I hadn't come home by nine o'clock, but the police never found me. I came home by myself to get more marbles. They had been so happy to see me. Maybe I should go home now, in case they were getting worried.

I didn't even have to go inside to hear what was going on. "Sophie, . . . I shouldn't have listened . . . America."

I turned around again. "C'mon, Bobbie."

Every day I wandered a little farther from the house. I discovered a farm close by. I asked Father about it. "Sure," he said, "I know them. That's the Droppers' farm. They have all those children."

"Eleven," I said. "They're very nice. I like Frits. He's in fourth grade, too, in the other school."

"Ies, she's spending too much time with them," Mother complained, "and I don't like it. From what Annie told me about Frits, he isn't very bright."

"That's not so," I yelled. "He knows plenty. How to climb trees, lots of things."

"That's all right. But maybe you shouldn't go there so often," Father said.

But where else could I go? From now on I wouldn't tell them everything. That would be better. At least at the Droppers', nobody was fighting. And nobody had a headache. Like at home.

Mother was right about the new house. We didn't even know what went on in town one night in October, not until the next day, when it was over and we were told about it.

Early in the morning when it was still dark, German

soldiers had gone through the streets in trucks. They drove slowly, with a list in their hands of the names and addresses of the Jewish men. With them on every truck was a Winterswijk policeman to show them the way. Most everybody was still sleeping. Many of the men were in their pajamas when they came to open the door. You can get dressed, they were told; but hurry; the truck is waiting, and we have more to do. The soldiers ran to the telephones to cut the wires, so nobody could be warned.

They came to our old house. The policeman didn't say that we had moved. After the soldiers realized that the house was empty, they ran across the street to the Gans family. They didn't take the parents. Only their big son.

"Father, where did the Germans take the men?" I asked.

Nobody knew for sure, he told me, but they were probably put on the train to Mauthausen, that place in Austria, where a lot of Jews had been sent before. German, Austrian, and Polish Jews. Mauthausen was the name of a jail camp. A concentration camp, people called it, where Hitler told his soldiers to beat Jews any time they felt like it.

Now why was I scared the next day when I went to school and saw three German soldiers in town? They wouldn't beat me. They ignored children. But I closed my eyes tightly when their boots were close to me. The sounds they made were so loud. Funny, why did I do it? I wasn't a man, like the Ganses' son.

Mrs. Gans came to our house with a yellow card. "Please," she said to Rachel, "what does it say? Our son wrote to us, but it's in German, and we can't read it." Her hand shook as she handed Rachel the card.

"I'm in Mauthausen since October 10," it said in typewritten letters. "I'm number 5562. Room B." In the left-hand corner were the words: "Write in German only. Add stamps for return letter."

"That Rachel. She's so capable," Mother said proudly.

I nodded.

Nine days later the letter that Rachel had written for Mrs. Gans came back from Mauthausen. UNKNOWN was stamped across the envelope.

"Funny, that they wouldn't remember him," Mother said.

The tree still talked, even to us outside of town. Jews weren't allowed to travel anymore, it said. But we would be allowed to travel in a truck, I thought. If the truck was one of theirs.

Father said he did not want to end up in Mauthausen, or in Germany, or in Poland where there were camps just like Mauthausen. "Listen," he said. "Phil and I have a plan. We might be able to get to Switzerland."

"How would you do that?" Mother asked.

"Somebody's going to drive us to the Swiss border. All Phil and I have to do is to get across it."

"What about us?" Mother asked.

"After we get to Switzerland, we'll send for you. And as soon as you arrive, I'm going to get the best doctors to look at you. Well, that's settled then. The day after tomorrow I'm leaving."

"But, Ies, you said it was a plan."

"Yes, yes." Then he noticed me. "Annie, why aren't you out playing? Listen, don't tell anybody about this. You understand?"

My head was spinning. Switzerland? With Hannie? Aunt Billa better not bother me too much about getting washed all the time.

I looked at Mother. Father's heavy winter coat was lying on her lap. With the tip of the scissors, she was opening the hem. When it was all done, she placed rolls of money in it and sewed it up again.

"You won't tell anybody, Annie, will you?"

I was getting annoyed at Father. Of course not. It was strange, though. How could he pay for things if he couldn't get at the money?

Very early in the morning, when it was still dark, Father waited by the back door for the man who would drive him to Switzerland.

"I'm too hot," Father complained, "with this heavy coat. Here he is. In a few days he may come for you. Be ready. I'll see you soon."

He slipped out of the house.

Two nights later, the doorbell rang. We ran down the stairs, picked up the suitcase we had packed, and opened the door. But it was not the man. Father stood by the door looking exhausted. They had not been able to get across the border, he said. It was too late for that.

I thought they could tell just by our faces. Rachel had said so. But maybe the star made it easier. Now everybody could tell by looking at our chests. *Jood* ("Jew") the star said, in black letters on a yellow background. And they weren't just ordinary letters. No, they had curlicues, especially the *d*.

Father was furious. "They even make you pay for these things," he shouted, "and textile coupons they want for them, too."

But the stars weren't so bad. I fingered mine. It made me look grown-up. Not all Jews had to wear the star, not children who weren't six yet. One little boy had a star on his tricycle. His father had had to make him one out of cardboard, because the little boy wasn't old enough for a real one made out of cloth. Like mine. And I had three more stars at home, real ones too. We needed that many, for we had to wear one all the time. Taking the star off one coat or jacket and sewing it on to another would have been a nuisance. If we could have just pinned it on our clothes. . . . But we weren't allowed to, the tree said so. No, I didn't mind about the star. Grandmother did, but she was old. She probably didn't like fancy things on her chest.

Many people wearing stars were at the station that afternoon, getting on the train. And many more were on the platform, staying behind. "Until after the war," the people in the train were shouting to the ones on the platform.

"Sure thing," the ones on the platform were shouting back.

The train was leaving for a Dutch camp, a labor camp, where work had to be done for Germany. Many Jews had received letters just like Rachel had, telling them they had been fired. A few men shook Father's hand. "De Leeuw, won't it be better to go to work for a little while than to sit around the house? It won't be for long, and they have told us we'll be treated well. So what can happen? Stay well, take care."

The tree had asked for Jewish volunteers. They were the people on the train.

"Fools," Father said angrily, "to just go. C'mon, Annie, let's not look any longer."

At home Rachel had set the table for four, because Mother no longer got out of bed.

"I don't understand why they went," Father said.

Oh, the men on the train.

"Annie, stop playing with that piece of bread," Rachel warned.

But I didn't want to eat. It tasted like sawdust. It even smelled like sawdust.

"Please eat up," Rachel said, "so I can do the dishes. I have so much work to do before three."

I knew why Rachel wanted to be ready by three. That's when we were allowed to shop. From three until five, every Jew ran through the streets from one store to the next. By three not much was left in the stores to buy. There was not even much to buy before three. Yesterday it had been Sini's turn to shop. She had come home without anything. Instead of shopping, she and Mr. Herschel had gone for a walk. Rachel had been furious.

I stuffed the last bite of food in my mouth. I was going to see whether Frits Droppers was home.

The tree said more volunteers were needed to work in labor camps. You could be as old as sixty. The Gans father was pleased he wasn't too old to go. Maybe someday he'd be sent out of Holland to another camp, he said. It had happened to a lot of people already. They had been put on the train to Poland. But maybe he'd be lucky enough to get sent to Austria and Mauthausen. And maybe he'd find his son there. Just in case, he took along his son's favorite sweater, the one with the cablestitching on the sleeves.

But there was so much work to be done, and not enough people volunteered. The tree no longer spoke nicely. "You must go," the notices said.

What would happen if you didn't? Father wasn't planning to go. "I'm looking for a place to hide," he told us. "I know many farmers, and one of them is bound to take us."

I stamped my foot. Mother had been wrong about the new house. Wrong. Wrong. Bobbie came running after me.

When I got to school the next morning, Mr. Herschel had not yet arrived. We stood outside, waiting for him, until Mr. Cohen, the other teacher, came. "You'd better go home," he said. "Mr. Herschel won't be back."

The first person I met when I came home was Sini. "How come you're home already?"

"German soldiers picked up Mr. Herschel. He won't be back. No more school."

Sini threw herself in a chair and started to cry. I didn't know what to say. Awkwardly I shuffled out of the room. Was that what happened if you didn't volunteer and they needed more workers? The truck would come? But Mr. Herschel had been working. He had not been sitting around the house like the father of Frits Droppers, who did nothing all day long. He should have to go, too.

There were many rumors that spring of 1942. The war would be over soon, some people said. Germany should never have invaded Russia. That country was just too cold for them and too big. German soldiers were also fighting in North Africa. "Sure, Italian soldiers are helping them there, but they don't amount to much."

How many soldiers did Hitler have? Enough to send them all over the world? Would they even get to Uncle Bram? Because the Germans were now at war with America too. Father said that was a terrible mistake. Hitler should have known better. He laughed when he said it, and I was not scared, not when he laughed like that.

There were other rumors, not such nice ones. Soon women could go to the labor camps too—if they felt like it. Mrs. Gans was already packed, waiting. Father said Rachel and Sini should start a nursery school in our house. Then the Germans would not expect them to go. They would be too busy doing useful work.

Every morning about ten children came on the backs of their mothers' bikes. I was waiting for them by the gate, wearing my star, just like the mothers. I took the children inside, and Sini showed them where to sit. I walked around checking on the pasting. "Look, the picture's getting all crooked, and don't wipe your sticky hands on your clothes. That's why we give you a rag."

Rachel shoved a little girl in my direction. "Annie, take this one to the bathroom."

"C'mon," I said, "this way. Hold my hand."

The summer turned out to be very nice. That poor Frits, having to go to school as a pupil. This was a school, too, where I was an assistant, and I was only ten.

"Today we're going for a walk in the woods. Line up here. Nice straight line, please." My voice even sounded like Rachel's. I was waiting for Rachel and Sini to come.

"Why are you wearing a rucksack?" I asked a little boy.

"I've got cookies in it," he answered.

When Rachel and Sini came, he took his neighbor's hand and hitched the rucksack up higher on his shoulders. "Let's go to Poland," he said. And away we walked, to pick flowers.

Mother's headaches became so bad that she had to go to the hospital. The hospital couldn't prepare kosher food for her, and Rachel went on making it at home. She took it to her every day in a wicker basket. At the hospital kitchen they gave Rachel yesterday's dirty dishes to bring home.

The only visitors Mother was allowed were the four of us and Grandmother. Grandmother sat at Mother's bed and didn't know what to say, except "Sophie, Sophie." But we didn't say much either. Everything made Mother nervous, especially news about the war. But what didn't have to do with the war? Frits Droppers didn't, and for the first time everybody listened to me when I talked about him. Until the nurse spoke to Father. "I'm sorry, Mr. de Leeuw, it doesn't affect only Mrs. de Leeuw. The two other Jewish patients we have can't receive any more visitors either."

"But this isn't possible," Father yelled. "What kind of new regulation is this? What harm is there in visiting sick people?"

"None," the nurse said. "I sympathize with you, but please don't shout. You're inside a hospital."

Silently we walked home. The tree had no business talking about Mother.

Still, every morning Rachel walked to the hospital to bring Mother's food. In yesterday's dishes Mother would put a note. They all said the same thing: "The days are so long. I miss you."

Father thought that Willy Bos's father might give me a permit to see Mother if I asked him.

"That NSB-er," Rachel said, "you don't want to ask favors of him."

But he was the mayor now, Father said, and why not try?

So I walked over to the town hall in my best summer dress. "Where's the mayor's office?" I asked a man. He pointed to a door upstairs.

I climbed the stairs that led to the first floor. Outside Dr. Bos's office I sat down on a bench with the others who wanted to see him. . . .

It should have been my turn now. That person should not have gone in ahead of me. He came only a few minutes ago. He shouldn't . . . I half got up. I tried to catch the attendant's attention, but I couldn't. I sat down again.

I was not going to stay on that bench all day just because I was a child! Maybe it was the star on my dress? But I had something to ask, too. Determinedly I got up.

"When will my turn come?" I asked the attendant. He didn't answer. Again I sat down.

"You." His voice made me jump. I walked into the office. Dr. Bos was sitting behind a desk. He went on reading, paying no attention to me. I came closer. Wasn't he ever going to stop? Maybe he didn't know I was here.

"Hello, Dr. Bos," I said.

He looked up from his papers. "Now there's a surprise. You used to go to school with Willy, didn't you. What's your first name again?"

"Annie."

"Right. Well, Annie, don't tell me that you have something that I can do for you? You don't think there's enough candy in the stores? Your mother should be thankful. How is she anyway?"

"She's in the hospital, and we can't visit her anymore. Can you give me a permit so that I can see her? Just me?"

He took a pad and wrote something on it. He tore a piece of paper off and gave it to me.

I read the note rapidly. "Thank you, Dr. Bos."

I ran all the way home. They would be proud of me.

They were—but not for long. Everybody was busy worrying. The tree asked for more and more volunteers. Young girls even. How much work could there be? Rachel secretly packed suitcases to take to the camp. Father wasn't allowed to know. He would have been mad. "We'll never go," he said. And every day he asked another farmer whether he could take us in. He had stopped dealing in cows.

"I'm not going to hide," Sini said. "Sitting somewhere in a room is no life."

Father told her she'd have no choice if he found a place. I wouldn't like to hide either. Maybe Rachel was right, and he wouldn't find anything. Then I could get on the train with my new little suitcase.

Some parents did go away to the camp or to a hiding place. Fewer and fewer children came to our school.

"Let's have a vacation," Rachel said to those who

still came, "so that everybody can rest up. Okay?"

The children nodded. That poor Frits. He kept saying he wished he were in our school, so that he could have a rest, too. Like me.

After dark, when we weren't supposed to be out anymore, we were busy, taking our furniture over to the Droppers'. It was a pity, Rachel said, to leave the furniture in the house for the Germans, in case we had to go to camp.

"Into hiding, you mean," Father said.

I mustn't tell Mother about it when I visited her. She wouldn't like to know. I couldn't talk to her about anything, not even about Frits because I might make a mistake and talk about his new furniture. I secretly looked at the clock when I went to see her. Thirty minutes is a long time. I didn't mind having to go back to Dr. Bos for three more permits when Mother became very sick. Now I would have company during my visits.

A few days later when Sini and I came back from the hospital, Rachel met us at the kitchen door. "One of us is no longer here," she said, "and it's Bobbie."

"Where is he?" I screamed.

"Father took him to a farmer who'll take good care of him."

I kicked the door as I went in. I hoped my foot would leave a mark. Bobbie was gone, and nobody had told me about it. Not until it was too late.

3

I⊤ was a lovely late summer day, and Father wanted me to come with him.

"Where are we going?" I asked.

"To the Abbinks. I'm going to talk to them about hiding."

"Be careful," Rachel warned, "and don't ride through town."

"I know, I know," Father said impatiently.

I knew, too. There were German soldiers in town. Now we couldn't ride bikes any more. We should have turned our bike in, but Father had refused.

"Let's go, Annie," Father said.

I climbed on the back of his bicycle.

It was warm. Father took a red handkerchief from his pocket and wiped his face. Bicycling must have been hard, the path was so narrow. On the right side were bushes; on the left, deep ruts caused by cart wheels. We were the only ones on the path. Most farmers were busy getting in their hay. But one passed us, sitting on his cart, the reins held loosely in his hands. The horse went slowly, head down, as if walking was almost too much trouble. Lazily the farmer raised a hand. "Morning," he said.

"Morning."

We went on. The mosquitoes were pesty that day. Impatiently I slapped at my face.

It was so quiet that I could hear a bluebottle fly buzz by.

"There it is," Father said, "and the farmer working in the field is Abbink."

"Morning."

"Hello, de Leeuw, and—eh?"

"Annie."

"Ja. Haven't seen you in a while, de Leeuw."

"I know. I'm not in business anymore. How's the haymaking coming?"

Abbink looked up. "If those clouds will just stay as white as they are now, we'll get the hay in on time." He put his fork down, and with the back of his arm he wiped the sweat off his face. "How's the wife?"

"Not very well."

"I never thought we'd be living in this mess, de Leeuw. I said to the wife the other night, I've got no stomach for work this summer. I don't know what I'm doing it for."

"What did the wife say?"

"She agrees."

"You know, Abbink, it won't be long before the Germans will pick us up and send us off."

"You think so?"

"Yes. Unless I can find people who'll take us in."

Father and Abbink looked each other straight in the eye.

"I wish I could help you, but my kids are too small. They wouldn't keep it a secret if we hid you." Abbink took off his cap and scratched his head.

Neither man said anything for a minute.

"De Leeuw, I'll tell you what. My wife's sister is married to a minister in town. He's a good man, and he knows a lot of people. I'll talk to him about you."

"I wish you would, Abbink."

"I don't know whether he can help, but I'll ask him to get in touch with you."

"Thanks. Well, you'd better get to work. I don't trust those clouds."

"Go in the house. My wife will give you some eggs."

On the way back to the bike, Father stopped to pick a cornflower. He stuck it in the buttonhole of his jacket. Absentmindedly he scratched a mosquito bite on the back of his hand. He waited for me to climb on the bicycle. "It's nice to be out with you again," he said.

It was. I looked up at him and smiled.

Carefully he got on the bicycle, holding the bag with eggs in one hand. "Rachel can make an omelet for Mother," he said softly. "She used to like them.".

A few days later a boy slipped a note under our door: "Be home tomorrow afternoon. Reverend Zwaal."

We were all home, waiting for him. But when he

came, Father and he went into the living room and left us in the kitchen. It took a long time for them to come out. When they did, Father had red blotches on his cheeks. He had a place, he said, near Rotterdam.

But Rotterdam was hours away, maybe even half a day! We'd have to go that far?

"One place?" Sini asked.

"Yes, and it has to be for me," Father said. "Mr. and Mrs. Hemmes—that's their name—want a man." And Reverend Zwaal would get him to Rotterdam, Father said.

"When are you going?" Rachel asked.

"After I've found a place for the three of you."

"Four of us," I said.

Father looked at me. "No, Annie. Mother's too sick to hide. She'll be safe in the hospital. Don't look so upset. Please? And don't tell her anything."

I swallowed. I said I wouldn't.

Early one morning in September, Uncle Phil rang our doorbell. He wanted to talk to us, he said, right away. "A Gentile friend of mine has offered to take Billa, Hannie, Grandmother, and myself in his house," he said.

"Where?" Father asked.

"A couple of hours from here by bicycle."

But he wasn't going to accept, Uncle Phil said, because Aunt Billa didn't want him to.

"Why doesn't she?" Father asked.

"They won't keep a kosher household for her," Uncle Phil said.

We all looked at him. His face was red, the part that I could see. He had come, he explained, to ask Father whether he would like to talk to his friend. Maybe we could stay in his house.

After Uncle Phil left, a man we had never seen before got off a bicycle in front of our house. He looked through the kitchen window.

Rachel opened it. "Who are you looking for?" she asked.

"Ies de Leeuw," said the man. "I'm Gerrit Hannink, a friend of your uncle's."

Curiously I looked at him. He was tall, his shoulders were bent. Together Father and he went into the living room. The door closed.

When Mr. Hannink had gone, Father called us in. "Come, come, hurry." Now we had a place, too, he said. All three of us would stay in Mr. Hannink's house. Miss Kleinhoonte, Rachel's and Sini's old high-school teacher, would plan with Mr. Hannink how we would get to Usselo, where he lived.

"I'm not going," Rachel said suddenly.

"What's the matter with you?" Father asked.

"Who's going to cook Mother's food?"

We all looked at Rachel. What about Mother's food? She would have to eat the hospital food, Father said. But Rachel said she wouldn't go. One of us must stay to look after Mother.

"I won't have it," Father shouted. "You'll go when

Sini and Annie do. Soon you'll have to leave Winterswijk anyway. You can't do anything for Mother. Nobody can. Why risk your life?"

Father was stamping up and down the room. But Rachel wouldn't come to Usselo, she said, not until she absolutely had to.

Early in October Father received a letter in the mail. By next week, the letter said, your family must go to a Dutch work camp. Report at the station. But they might not take us to a work camp. That letter could be lying. Father said so. Lots of times the train rode right on to Germany, or Austria or Poland, to those concentration camps. Didn't Rachel hear what Father said? She didn't want to get beaten by Hitler's soldiers! Then wouldn't she have to come with Sini and me?

The next day somebody would come to take Father to Mr. and Mrs. Hemmes. That afternoon Father and I went to the hospital to see Mother, but we said nothing about the letter or the Hemmeses. On the way home I held his hand tightly.

"Annie, you be a good girl in Usselo. Miss Kleinhoonte will give you some textbooks. You learn something while you're in hiding. Rachel or Sini will help you. After the war you and I'll go to the farmers again . . . buy cows."

I held his hand even tighter.

We got up early the next morning, long before Father was supposed to leave. On my way downstairs I heard "Rachel . . . must . . . Usselo." Poor Father was always fighting. When I came in, he stopped. "Let's go," he mumbled, pulling his fingers one by one. A few of them made cracking noises.

"Please, Father," Rachel said.

"Don't sound like your mother." Father's voice was sharp.

Nobody said anything.

"Well, okay, I'm going. It isn't quite time yet, but Reverend Zwaal said the man might come a little early . . . you never know. . . . Take the money I gave you to go to Usselo. . . . Take care." He put on his coat and hugged us. "After the war. . . ." He stopped abruptly, picked up his suitcase, and left.

The door closed with a bang.

Just before noon a frail old lady came. It was Miss Kleinhoonte. "Your father has arrived safely," she said. "I just talked to Reverend Zwaal. Now I'll tell you how you're to get to the Hanninks'." She turned to Rachel. "Your father told me about you. Do you still want to stay?"

Yes, Rachel wasn't ready to go yet, she said. She would certainly stay until next week, till the deadline.

"You shouldn't. But as long as you feel that way, Reverend Zwaal wants you to spend every night at his house."

Then Miss Kleinhoonte said that Sini was to bicycle

to Usselo the next morning. Sini was to dye her hair and dress as a farm girl. Mr. Hannink would meet her just outside of Usselo. "Don't show that you know him. Just follow him. After a little while he'll turn into a drive. That's the drive to his house. Go into the garage and wait."

I listened excitedly. What about me?

I was to get a boy's haircut, Miss Kleinhoonte said, and wear a sailor suit.

"But I'll look like a boy! What if I see somebody who knows me." That could happen. I sucked in my breath.

"Let's hope they won't recognize you. That's the whole idea," said Rachel.

"At eight o'clock tomorrow morning, walk to the bus stop near my house," Miss Kleinhoonte went on. "At eight sixteen the bus will arrive. It will say Winterswijk-Enschede on the front. Get on it and buy a ticket to Enschede."

But wasn't I going to Usselo? I asked. I was, but not right away, Miss Kleinhoonte said. Usselo was such a small town that people would stare at me if I got off the bus. It was safer to get off in Enschede, which was a big town.

"In Enschede, at the last stop, a young girl will be waiting for you. Her name is Dini Hannink. Get on the back of her bicycle, and she'll take you to her house in Usselo."

So much to remember. And I'd look like a boy. What if I saw Frits?

It was time for us to go and see Mother, Sini said. I didn't want to go. Shouldn't she know that we wouldn't be coming tomorrow to see her? Or the day after? Or, or . . . no, no!

"Why didn't Father come to see me this morning?" Mother asked.

Sini bent over her bed. "He had to go into hiding," she whispered. "But he has it so good. He's in a fine hotel. The food is supposed to be great."

I blushed. How could Sini lie? But Mother smiled.

When the thirty minutes were over, Sini left the room first.

"Annie," Mother said, "remember that candy machine by the station?"

I nodded.

"Do you think that's still working?"

"Probably."

"Here's a twenty-five-cent piece for you. On the way home you can buy something."

I grabbed the money out of her hand and ran. I didn't want her to see my tears.

Outside Sini was waiting for me.

"How long is Mother going to be sick?" I asked.

"Nobody knows," she said, "but she's going to die. And it's probably going to happen soon."

I found I wasn't surprised.

At home Rachel was waiting with a bottle of peroxide in her hand. "First wash your hair," she said to Sini. I sat down on the bed to watch. Sini was pretty.

Her hair was long and shiny, but black—the wrong color.

Rachel poured some peroxide in a glass, then filled the glass up with water. She emptied it on Sini's hair. We waited speechlessly. And after a little while, something wrong was happening. Right in front of our eyes, Sini's hair began to turn red, rusty barbed-wire red. Dull, lifeless red. Rachel stopped.

With a jerk Sini lifted her head, splashing water on us. She pushed the hair out of her eyes and looked. "This won't do," she said furiously. "Look, it's awful."

I pointed at her eyebrows. "They are still black."

With angry movements Sini pulled most of her eyebrows out. The skin above her eyes was red and swollen. It must have hurt. I shouldn't have mentioned them.

My turn came. Rachel put a towel around me, picked up the scissors, and started to cut. Tufts of hair fell down. So many. When they stopped coming, I walked over to the mirror: two frightened green eyes looked at me from a very round face. I hated round faces. It hadn't been that bad when my hair was long. I tried sucking in my cheeks; it didn't help.

I didn't believe Sini and Rachel when they told me how cute I looked. In bed I pulled the sheet over my head.

When I woke up, it was still dark. I got out of bed to see whether it was raining. I stuck my hand out the window and waited. Not a drop. I turned around and switched on the light: four o'clock. I sat down on the bed. In the corner by the window had been a table, but we had given it to the Droppers. Frits probably used it for his homework—for school.

I heard noises coming from the kitchen. Sini and Rachel must be up. I went down to see. Sini was taking the star off her coat with a pair of scissors. She snipped at the six corners until the star fell off. Her face was flushed.

"Now I have to get dressed," she said. "Wait till you see me come down."

"Rachel," I asked, "when are you coming to Usselo?"

"Soon," she answered.

"Rachel, you know, that truck." What if she was home and the truck came for her?

She told me I shouldn't worry. She was twenty-five— and that was the reason she knew so much.

"Will we come back?" I asked. "From Usselo?"

That she didn't know, Rachel said.

Not everybody who hid came back. A group of Jews who had been hiding for weeks in a Winterswijk swamp had been caught. It wasn't nice to hide, the Germans said. The group was sent to Poland. Maybe they'd come back after the war. Could be. Rachel didn't know. Anyway, those people had hid themselves. Those Jews had not had a Gentile family to take care of them—like we did.

Sini came down the stairs dressed as a farm girl. A scarf covered almost all her hair. She put a bundle of clothes on the back of the bike. "I can't bear to stay in all day," she said in a funny voice. "Why do I have to? I don't even look Jewish. Without the star how can anyone tell!"

Rachel walked away.

"Goodbye, Sini. See you later today," I said.

Sini wheeled the bike out on the road and got on it. The church clock struck five.

Three hours later I left. I looked good, Rachel said. Gingerly I felt the hair underneath my cap. I turned around to wave once more, but Rachel had gone back into the house.

So nice! Rachel had let me take the new suitcase. I swung it back and forth. It was scary to look down on my clothes and not see the star. I walked faster. Have to be careful, can't very well run.

I started to whistle—songs I hadn't thought about since first grade. . . . First grade . . . ages ago . . . for babies. I stuck one hand in my pants' pocket and whistled louder. I had reached the outskirts of town.

It was crowded in the street, with people going to work, on bikes, on foot. As I turned left, I noticed straight ahead, coming toward me, somebody I knew—a neighbor from our old house in Winterswijk. He was on a bike. The distance between him and me became smaller, until he was next to me, looking at me, going slower, passing me, saying nothing, only turning his head to get another look.

Legs, go. Go. Up, stretch, down. And up and stretch

and down. What if he's going to report me? If anyone asked, I was to say I was Jan de Wit. It was a good Gentile name. Ha, who would believe me?

I shivered.

I looked back to see whether he was following me. No, but wasn't that Rachel, walking a block behind me? Yes. I stopped to wait for her, but she shook her head. She didn't want me to wait.

I got to the bus stop. Nobody else was there. I put the suitcase down and waited. A few minutes later a yellow bus appeared. What if it drove past?

I waved wildly. The bus slowed down, stopped. The door opened, and I walked up the steps, pushing the suitcase ahead of me. The door closed behind me.

"One way to Enschede, please."

When I looked out the window, I saw Rachel's back. She was on her way home.

4

I SAT down in the back of the bus, suitcase in front of me. Next to me was an elderly woman. I moved as far away from her as I could. Had I ever been on a bus before? Maybe Sini would remember. I certainly had never bought my own ticket before. Carefully I took the ticket out of my pocket and studied it. So many little holes.

About half an hour outside of Winterswijk, the bus came to a sudden halt. Everyone stretched his neck to see why. The driver opened the door, and several Dutch soldiers came in. "Stay in your seats. Routine control. Open your bags."

What if they open my suitcase! What will I say? That those clothes are mine? They can't be; they're girls' clothes. Why didn't Rachel tell me what to say! I squirmed in my seat.

One of the soldiers came to the back of the bus. "That yours, little boy?"

Innocently I looked up at him. "Oh—the suitcase? It's full of girls' clothes I'm taking to my aunt."

He nodded and went on. I wiped my wet hands on my knee socks. A few minutes later they left, carrying a killed chicken. The man they had taken it from looked mad. "That's what they meant by routine control?" he complained.

The bus started up again.

The scenery outside was the same as that around Winterswijk—flat, meadows, cows. I wanted to ask my neighbor whether she knew where Usselo was, but I didn't. What if she questioned me? I kept looking for the town. About twenty minutes later we reached Enschede. We had gone through Usselo, and I had missed it.

I stayed on the bus until the driver announced the last stop. I climbed down.

Somebody tapped me on the shoulder. Frightened, I turned around.

"I'm Dini Hannink. What's your name?"

"Annie de Leeuw."

"Get on the back of the bike. Okay? Let's go."

With one hand I held the suitcase; with the other, I hung on to Dini's back.

So this was Usselo. It seemed to be nothing but a road. Here and there were a few farms, a bakery.

"See that house off the road, to your right?" Dini asked. "That's where I live." She rode into the garage.

I slid off the bike. I waited, holding my suitcase. While Dini was putting her bicycle away, a long-haired white dog ran in. I laughed. Great. I followed the dog out of the garage, but Dini ran after me.

"Get back, Annie, there's the road. Somebody might see you."

See me? I bit my lips. Ashamed, I stepped back. When Dini had made sure that nobody was watching us, we walked to the house where Mr. and Mrs. Hannink were waiting downstairs. They took me to a room upstairs—where Sini was sitting on the edge of the bed.

Silently we looked out of the window. It faced the backyard. We looked at the bedspread. It was crocheted. We looked around some more. At the door— it was closed—and at each other.

Sini began studying her watch. She frowned, shook it, put it to her ear, and sighed.

Did we have to stay in the room all day and all night? Sini had been right. This was no life.

Unpacking didn't take long, but it made us quarrel. Sini wasn't fair. I needed space for my clothes, too. That drawer wasn't only hers. Glumly I stared out the window all afternoon, thinking about it. When Sini said goodnight, I didn't answer her. Why should I? But much later, when I looked at her through my eyelashes and saw that her eyes were open, I stuck out my hand.

Maybe she was right. Her clothes were bigger; they'd need more space than mine.

When would we have to get up? Sini said it didn't matter, but we couldn't stay in bed all day, could we?

I opened the curtains. I hadn't realized yesterday how many fruit trees were in the back of the house. I tried counting them. I got to eleven, but there were more. I noticed branches that didn't belong to the tree trunks I could see. I walked all the way over to the right side of the window and pushed my cheek against it. I closed one eye so that I could concentrate better on what was on the left. I still couldn't see. Irritatedly I went back to bed.

"I wonder when the Hanninks get up," I said.

"We should offer to clean the upstairs," Sini answered.

"They'll have to get up soon. Dini has to go to school early."

"You'll have to help me dust."

"Doesn't Mr. Hannink go to work? What time is it?"

"Annie, stop asking me that question! Here." Sini jumped out of bed, took her watch off, and put it on the commode. "Now you can see for yourself."

Somebody walked across the hall. The lock of the bathroom clicked. I ran over to the watch and announced: "Seven o'clock. Now we know when they get up."

Sure, they had to get up. They had places to go. I used to have places to go, too. Before the tree said all those things, we used to go to a hotel by the ocean. Maybe we'd go back there next summer. On hot days Father used to roll up his pants and walk to the edge of the water. "C'mon, Sophie," he'd call, "it's not too cold. Can't be—not with all those people in the water."

But Mother always stayed in her chair, smiling. Father would move a little closer to the water, closer, closer . . . until his foot touched it. He'd withdraw it right away. But he went again, bravely. When a wave approached, he'd go back rapidly. Like what-do-you-call-them? Sandpipers.

A few minutes later he'd join Mother again. "C'mon, Sophie, let me pull you in."

Mother would laugh, but not go.

"You're missing something, Sophie," he'd say, "the water's just right."

That would make Mother laugh even louder. Father would pull up his chair next to hers, and they'd talk. Not yell. Not shout. Nice.

Would Rachel tell Mother we were in a good hotel, too? "Sini, d'you think she has?"

"Maybe so."

"But would Mother believe her, Sini?"

"I wouldn't be surprised," Sini answered. "Mother never understood that Hitler is after the Jews. If she had, we would've gone to America when Father wanted to."

I remembered: "Sophie . . . let's . . . America"; screaming voices.

"Did you know that Father was scared, Annie?"

Father scared? "No, Sini." I was almost yelling.

"Sure, or he'd be in Winterswijk now risking his life, not Rachel. Haven't you ever seen him scared before?"

How could Sini say those things? "No."

"I have. Whenever a farmer didn't want to pay, I

had to go to collect the money. Now I shouldn't have had to do that. But Father was too scared to ask for it himself. Then he'd get mad at me if I lost some of it on the way home," Sini said angrily.

I glared at her. Well, she should have been more careful. He had been right. And why did talking about money remind her of my math textbook?

"Not this early, Sini." We hadn't even had breakfast yet!

Places to go. Mrs. Hannink had told us that Mr. Hannink was building an underground hiding place in the backyard. "For you girls to stay in if it's too dangerous in the house."

Maybe I'd get to go there some time, and stay for a while.

Smilingly I looked at Sini. She'd probably like that too. But maybe she hadn't heard. She was pacing back and forth, shaking her fists at the window. "Annie, how much longer? I have to get out—out!"

But we had only been in the room a day and a night.

"I think I can take it if it's just for the winter. But in the spring, Annie, if we're still here in May, I'll go crazy. You hear me?"

I heard. That's when I wanted to get out, too. I'd climb trees with Frits again.

"I have to have a tan in the summer. I look terrible without one. Annie, answer me." What was I supposed to say? "Tell me honestly. Am I ugly with this red hair and no eyebrows?"

I studied her critically. Sini stood in front of me, waiting for my answer. "You're pretty. Really. I wish I looked like you."

"Come here, silly. We'll manage, you and I."

It would be nice when Rachel came. I stealthily passed the commode and glanced at the watch. Maybe Mrs. Hannink would let the dog come upstairs. That would be nice. When she and Dini came in to talk to us, I asked her. "Sure," she said, and Kees came. He wagged his tail at us, licked us, jumped on us . . . then ran over to the door. Out. Bobbie wouldn't have done that. He would've stayed with me.

Unhappily I looked out the window. "You're lucky you can stay in today," Dini said. "It's awful out. I wish I could stay up here with you." But right after she said that she left—to go to school. I'd even go to school and like it, if I could get out.

Dini was right about the weather today. The wind was howling. Once in a while an abandoned apple was swept off a tree. Plop. It didn't fall straight down. It was first thrown against nearby branches or the tree trunk. Plop. The apple would be bruised by the time it got to the ground. It would have cracks in it. Juice would ooze out. If nobody picked it up for a day or so, it would turn brown where it was bruised. Ants would walk back and forth in the cracks. If you left it any longer, the whole apple would turn a dull brown. Rot. Smell. Even the bugs would lose interest. Leaves would cover it. Somebody would step on it. Squash it. End it.

I picked up a book and turned some of the pages. What a boring story.

Mother died. Miss Kleinhoonte called Mr. Hannink to tell him. We had known Mother would die soon. But when he told us, it hurt just the same. After Mr. Hannink left, Sini and I sat on the bed, close together. We cried.

I wondered whether Grandmother knew. She probably did, unless she had already gotten on that train with Uncle Phil, Aunt Billa, and Hannie.

Now Rachel would come. She'd have to. She was probably getting ready right now.

But she didn't come, and she wasn't going to, either. She had gone to somebody else's house instead, Mr. Hannink said, and we didn't even know why. Reverend Zwaal hadn't wanted to talk about it over the telephone. To think that Sini and I had even put our clothes together so Rachel could have her own drawer.

"My God, why does it have to be me who's stuck with you?" Sini cried.

"I wish it weren't you either," I said furiously. "I'd rather be with Rachel any day." But after a minute I walked over to Sini and sat on her lap. I buried my head in her neck and sobbed. "Don't," she said, "I'll take care of my little sister."

Sini picked up the calendar Mrs. Hannink had given us and hung it over our bed. Today was the twelfth of November. How long had we been here? I tried to remember, but I couldn't, and didn't dare ask Sini. Could she be right that we might be here forever? A long time ago there had been a war between Holland and Spain, she had told me, which lasted for eighty years. Eighty. Let's see. I'd be ninety. And Sini would be one hundred. There she was, standing by the bed with a pencil in her hand. With hard angry movements she crossed off the first eleven days of November. Eleven deep black crosses. Would she mark off the twelfth, too? She shouldn't. Today wasn't over yet. Wasn't it easy? All you had to do was to cross them off. Every day of the month. You could even do it ahead. Why not?

Nervously I walked around the room, tripping over the rug every time I came near it. I pushed my face against the window. "Sini, come here. I think I can see the hiding place."

"Where?"

"Through those two trees. See how the ground is a little elevated there?" Could you stand up in it? I wished I were there now, so that I could talk about it later. I would, too: "You'll never guess where I was. In a place under the ground. Yes, sure, under the ground. A grave? No, of course not. Would I have come back from a grave? Well, actually it was a little bit like a grave, I guess. Only you went in alive."

And Frits would look at me with his mouth wide open. Dumb thing, he was. Darn, why couldn't I go out and take a look at it?

Some people were lucky, like the two Jews who were

in the backyard now. Mr. Hannink had brought them to the hiding place last night. "They'll stay there," he said, "until I can take them to their real place."

As if that wasn't a real place. Why didn't he take us there, and let them stay up here? And why was he always getting new Jews anyway? Well, I didn't mind, but they were the ones who got to live in the cave for a while, until he found them a home. They probably didn't even want a home. I didn't want one. I wanted a cave!

November became December, and every day I hoped it would snow. And one day it did.

"Sini, come to the window."

Tiny white snowflakes were whirling down. I tried to follow one. I lifted my head, singled one out, and moved my eyes with it. Before the flake hit the window, I had to step away. Watching it made me dizzy.

"Sini, let me out for this one time. It's snowing!" I looked up at her. What would happen if I went out just once. "Sini, please."

"You know you can't, but I'll let you touch the snow," she said.

She opened the window a little bit. I stuck my hand out far enough to catch some snowflakes. A pity, they melted as soon as they landed on me. I sat down on the bed. I heard Dini coming up the stairs. She must be covered with snow. She probably had some stuck on her shoes.

"Shall I make you a snowman?" she asked.

"What do you mean?" But she was already on her

way down the stairs. I walked over to the window.

There she was, rolling a ball of snow through the backyard. She looked up. I pushed my face against the window. The ball was getting bigger and bigger. It wasn't perfectly shaped though. My hands fumbled with the curtain. There. She had put the ball in place underneath the window. She pushed it against a tree. Right. That's what I would have done, too. A smaller ball for the head. What a funny shape! The snowman was going to have a pointed head.

"Sini, come and look. It's so much fun." But he should be wearing a hat. The ones I used to make always did. Where is Dini? Maybe she went inside to get one. Please. Yes, she has one. I laughed. Waved at her. Great.

"Are your hands very cold?" I mouthed the words at her when she looked up. She didn't understand. I spread my hands out, brought them to my face, blew on them, stuck them under my arms. Yes?

She nodded.

As soon as I woke up the next morning, I opened the curtain. The snowman was still there, but he was smaller. The hat had dropped over his eyes. He looked sad.

Christmas came, although Sini had said it never would. The Hanninks had company downstairs. "You can't make any noise," Mrs. Hannink said, "until after they've gone." Of course not. I understood. Absentmindedly I played with the chair next to me.

"Don't, Annie," Sini warned.

Don't what? And I played with it again, tipping it back and forth.

"You heard what Mrs. Hannink said."

"Sure," I answered in a whisper, my hand on the chair. And then it fell.

Sini grabbed my arm. Not a sound came from downstairs. Then Mr. and Mrs. Hannink started to laugh loudly. What was so funny? I thought irritably.

I didn't think that any longer after Mr. Hannink talked to me when the company had left. Nobody should suspect that there were people upstairs, he said. They might tell the Germans who would come to look. If they found us, they'd punish the Hanninks and take us away to Mauthausen or to a camp in Poland. My lips trembled. Would I never stop hearing about those trucks?

But he was suspected anyway, Mr. Hannink said a few evenings later. And it had nothing to do with the chair. He had taken a Jewish child from one family to another. Everything had gone well, he said. It was dark, and the child hadn't said a word. But on the way back, Mr. Hannink had been followed by a German soldier.

"I don't think he followed me all the way home," Mr. Hannink said, "and maybe I imagined the whole thing, but it will be better if you go away for a little while. If nothing happens within a week or so, you can come back."

"Where are we going?" Sini asked.

I looked at her. Was she crying?

To a farm nearby, Mr. Hannink said, only he couldn't take us there until tomorrow night. In the meantime, we'd have to stay in the hiding place out back, just in case the house was searched.

Sini and I packed our things. At last I was going to the cave. "Sini, I'm so excited. I wish we could stay longer than one day. D'you think it's dark in there or. . . ."

"Stop it," Sini said wearily. "Do you know what day it is? New Year's Eve. Ha, ha, New Year's Eve. Well, let's not take the calendar. Maybe we'll get a new one next week. For 1943."

Impatiently I looked at the watch, which Sini let me wear. Mr. Hannink had said he'd be back in half an hour. Where was he? I was ready. I rocked back and forth on the chair. C'mon, let's go. It's time.

Quietly we followed Mr. Hannink downstairs. Mrs. Hannink gave us a bag. "A couple of sandwiches. And, girls, I'll see you in a week. Two at the most."

"So long, Mrs. Hannink."

It was cold outside. I shivered. We stayed close behind Mr. Hannink. At last I was going to find out what the hiding place looked like.

Mr. Hannink stood still. He bent down and moved some branches away with his hands. An opening appeared. He shone a flashlight into it. "Follow me," he whispered.

Sini went first, holding on to my hand. Why was it

so dark? I licked my lips. They felt dry. Gingerly I stepped forward and down.

Mr. Hannink shone the flashlight ahead. We were in a long, narrow room. The sides and ceiling were covered with wooden strips. Blankets lay on the floor. I pushed them away with my foot to see what was underneath them. Wood, too. In the corner was a chamber pot.

"Tomorrow night, around eleven I'll come for you. Well, good night. Keep the flashlight on as long as you want to. There are more batteries in the box."

Mr. Hannink went outside. He put the branches back in place.

It wasn't cold inside. The room smelled only a little dank. We put the flashlight on the floor between us. It lit up the area right by our feet and the end of the room.

"Let's wrap ourselves in a blanket. Annie, here, I'll help you. What time is it?" I moved my arm toward the light. "Nine o'clock."

Where were we going tomorrow night? They were farmers, and their name was Oosterveld, but who were they? What if they weren't nice? I put my head in my hands. That could be. It was a good thing we'd only stay for a week, in case they weren't.

Now that I was here I didn't like the cave. There was nothing special about a hole in the ground. How many hours did we have to stay? Twenty-four? I wanted to leave now. I walked to the circle of light at the end of the hole.

"Annie, what are you doing?"

"Nothing. I'll be right back."

Could the ceiling come down? I lifted my hands. Right over my head were a lot of crisscrossed branches. They felt cold. I tried poking my finger through them. What would happen if somebody stepped on them? And fell? What would we say?

I walked back to Sini. She was hiding her face. Hesitantly I sat down next to her. "Want to stay up till midnight?" I asked her.

"Why? What's there to do until then? You want me to wish you a Happy New Year? Fine New Year. If it weren't for this miserable war, I'd be at a party tonight. I would, too. I used to be popular. Did you know that? Boys were always asking me out. Those were the days. I was somebody then. New Year's Eve. Even last year was better. I stayed home, but it wasn't bad. Rachel made New Year's fritters. We all sat in Mother's room, eating them. We stayed up till midnight. Mother, too. Father said it was one of the nicest New Year's Eves he remembered. Even you stayed up."

I nodded. I had.

"But look at me now. Here I am, twenty years old. And miserable. See what I'm wearing? See what my hair looks like? I'm glad I can't go out tonight. I wouldn't dare. Well, nobody would've asked me the way I look. No, little sister, I can't see staying awake until midnight. The sooner this night is over, the better."

She took my hand. "Annie, what's the first thing you want to do when we're free?"

I thought. "Get a bike and go for a ride—a long one.

No, first I'll pick up Bobbie. Father will take me in his car, a new one. And I want to go—you know where I want to go next?—to the store, to get ice cream. Vanilla. And I won't have to wait till three o'clock either. I'll be the first one there. In the morning. When they open. The minute the door unlocks, I'll step in, put my money on the counter, and say 'One double vanilla cone.' That's what I'll do."

Sini laughed. She was glad I was with her, she said. It made things easier.

Being in that place was impossible though. I never knew twenty-four hours had so many minutes. And seconds. Maybe we should go to sleep. Time would go faster.

At last the branches came off the doorway. "Girls, are you ready?"

Ready? I stuck my head out of the opening and breathed in. Yes, I was ready.

The soldiers hadn't come, Mr. Hannink said. "But that could be a trick. Maybe they're going to wait until I no longer expect them. I know them. Come."

It was very dark. Several times we tripped. Mr. Hannink took my hand. "You hold on to Sini. Once we're on the road, walking will be easier."

He held our suitcase in his other hand. We came to the end of the backyard. Mr. Hannink went on the road first.

It was lighter now, easier to see. Also more dangerous. Mr. Hannink walked rapidly for a few seconds to get ahead of us, then slowed down. Soon we came to the corner of the street where the bakery was. I tried to see it.

"Come, Annie," Sini whispered.

Mr. Hannink had already turned the corner. There was no sidewalk, only grass. We walked a little faster. Nobody was on the street. The only sound came from high-flying airplanes. A lot of them were out tonight. They probably came from England, or all the way from America, to bomb factories in Germany. Sometimes they were chased by German planes, and you could hear them shooting at each other.

The last thing we'd need now was an air-raid alarm. Terrible sound that was. It went right through you. We'd have to get off the streets, too. Did Sini think the same thing I did? That we were walking outside for the first time in two months? Scary. I made sure I didn't let go of her hand.

Mr. Hannink stopped, looked behind him, then beckoned us to come closer. He pointed to the right. Then he opened a low wooden gate, went through it, and so did we. A house. He turned around again and put the suitcase by us. "Stay here for a minute. This is it." He walked a few feet, knocked at a door, and went in.

Footsteps, Mr. Hannink's, coming back. "Okay, you can come."

Mr. Hannink went in the same door again. We followed. The door closed. Somebody turned the key, then switched on the light.

5

THESE are the Oostervelds. And this," Mr. Hannink said, "is Sini. That's Annie."

Sini and I stepped forward. I stuck out my hand to an old lady. "How do you do, Mrs. Oosterveld."

The old lady laughed. "God-o-god-o-god, Mrs.!"

I turned to the younger woman and said the same thing, but hesitantly this time.

It made her laugh, too.

"We're plain people," the man said. "Just call us by our first names. I'm Johan. That's Dientje—she's the wife—and that's my mother. You can call her *Opoe* [Granny]. So," Johan said, "you'll take 'em back in a week?"

"Yes, two at the most," Mr. Hannink answered.

"Ja, ja, okay. Don't forget."

Johan turned off the light and unlocked the door. Mr. Hannink slipped through it.

"Now, let's see you. Goodness, you're a little thing,"

Opoe said. "You can't be very old. How old are you?"

"I'm almost eleven."

"What's the matter with your hair?" she asked Sini. "Got two colors. It didn't grow that way, did it?"

Sini explained.

"Boy, o boy, isn't that something! Dyed hair. What's next?"

I looked around. We were obviously in the kitchen. In the middle of the room stood a wood-burning stove with wooden shoes standing around it. There were two windows. Both of them had dark shades, pulled down. I moved closer to the stove. Nice and warm.

"Want a cup of coffee?" Dientje went to the cupboard and got two cups, then to the stove for the coffeepot.

"Dientje," Sini said, "I don't think Annie should have coffee."

"She sick?"

"No, but she's kind of young."

"Coffee never hurt anyone," Dientje answered calmly and poured two cups.

"This kind won't hurt her," Opoe said. "Hasn't got many real coffee beans in it. It's mostly junk. Additions. Dientje, I always told you to store up on coffee when you still could, but you didn't listen."

"What are you talking about," Dientje mumbled. She looked annoyed.

I picked up my cup with both hands and sipped slowly. The coffee tasted kind of bad, but I felt very grown-up.

I looked at Dientje. She had such big hands. I stared at them with awe. Johan's hands were big, too, and red. So was his face. On top of his head brown-gray hair grew straight up. He didn't look a bit like Opoe, who was short, round, with old gnarled hands. On her right temple was a wart. She was wearing a long black dress with long sleeves, and over it a black apron with gray flowers. Embarrassed I looked away. It wasn't polite to stare.

Sini and Johan were talking—about the war. "You know something. I never handed in my radio."

The Oostervelds had a radio, too? Nobody would listen to me again. "Ssht," they'd say.

"Not me. At night I listen to a Dutch broadcast from England. That's for the real news. Those damn newspapers never tell you a damn thing. Nothing but lies."

"Damn" twice in one sentence! I forgot that I was annoyed.

"I'll give you an example. The papers tell us how well the German army's doing in Russia. When they have to give up a town, they say they did so for tactical reasons. Tactical reasons, shit."

"Johan, please." Dientje looked anxiously at him. "Don't talk that way. What'll the girls think of you?"

"I don't care. Now the radio tells you differently. A defeat is a defeat. And the Germans are having plenty of them right now in Russia."

"Johan, the girls must be tired. Let them go to bed."

"Okay, Ma. Let's go upstairs."

We went through the kitchen door and came into a biggish room with a plush tablecloth, straight chairs, and portraits.

"Here, the stairs are behind this door to the left."

We all went up.

"Now this is where you'll be," Johan said.

"Just for two weeks," Dientje added.

"Ja, ja, woman," Johan said.

The room was small, with a stove in it, two chairs, and a big bed. Johan pointed at the bed. "Annie'll sleep in there with Dientje and me." It wasn't wide enough for Sini, too, he said. "She'll have to sleep on the floor on a mattress. If anybody comes to the house during the night, Annie can jump out of bed, and I'll put Sini's bedding on top of ours so it doesn't show that we've got two extra people sleeping in here."

"And then where do the girls go, Johan?" Dientje asked.

"Under the bed, woman."

"Good night, girls." Opoe was standing in the doorway. She went into her room, next to ours.

"I told you we're plain people," Johan said, "not like those fancy Hanninks."

"Johan, it's late," Dientje warned.

"We haven't got a bathroom in the house. There's an outhouse, but you can't get there. You use a chamber pot, and Dientje'll empty it."

He took off his socks, corduroy pants, and shirt. He got into bed. Dientje moved next to him. "Johan, move over. Annie needs more space."

I climbed in next to Dientje. She lifted her hand over her head and pulled a cord. Instantly the room became dark. I looked over the edge of the bed to where I knew Sini was. I lowered my hand until I touched her face. "Good night."

"Good night, little one."

Along the edges of the shade a little light crept through. From the far side of the bed came Johan's snoring. "Johan, don't snore so. What'll the girls think?"

The Oostervelds were nice.

In what seemed to be the middle of the night, the alarm clock went off. Opoe called from her room, "Johan, get up."

Nothing happened. I pulled the feather comforter over my ears. Dientje lifted herself up on an elbow and looked at the alarm. "Johan, what's the matter with you? Didn't you hear the alarm go off?"

"That's all you women ever tell me. Get up, Johan. Go milk the cows, Johan. Feed the pigs, Johan. Why don't you get up too, eh, and help me?"

"Quit it, you know I don't feel well in the morning."

"Awright, woman, I'm up." He lifted the comforter. Goodnaturedly he slapped Dientje's thigh and stepped out of bed. He felt around for his clothes. "Can't find my socks. Got to turn the light on."

"Johan, you're late." Opoe came in, dressed.

"Stop nagging. The cows'll wait."

But he left the room. Opoe went downstairs with him. Dientje turned the light off again and moved to Johan's side of the bed. It was nice to have more space. I closed my eyes. From downstairs came the noise of the stove being lit and the hushed voices of Opoe and Johan.

The Oostervelds got up early. At least, two of them did. An hour later Dientje went downstairs.

They were talking when they came upstairs a few minutes later. "Johan, it doesn't make sense for those few days. Johan, you hear?"

"Leave'm alone," Opoe said. "He's already worked hard."

They walked in. This room was at the front of the house, Johan explained, and the window faced the street. "We can't keep the shade down during the day. We never did before. Groothuis across the street would think something was peculiar, but for Godsake don't go near the window."

Opoe and Dientje nodded.

"We have another bedroom in the back," Johan went on, "but it's too cold there in the winter, and we can't heat it. That one would be good in the summer."

"But Johan," Dientje stammered, "they're only staying for a few weeks."

"You'd have more freedom there," he went on calmly. "Ma, where you going?"

"Downstairs to get the girls some breakfast."

Obviously Dientje hadn't stocked up on real tea either. It tasted funny. Un-tealike. But it was hot. Nice.

Johan got a tin box from his pocket and a package of cigarette paper. Carefully he pulled out a piece of paper. He opened the box, took a fingerful of tobacco from it, and distributed it inside the cigarette paper. Deftly he rolled the paper around the tobacco, licked it, pinched off the ends. He stuck the cigarette in his mouth and lit a match. He inhaled deeply. "I'm growing my own tobacco. Can't smoke the stuff they're selling."

"Johan, you've got to go to work," Dientje complained.

He didn't answer her. Opoe was staring at Sini's skirt. She came closer and touched it. "Fine material. Must've been bought before the war. What you get now's junk. D'you know that I haven't bought any clothes for over ten years?"

"Ma, you complaining?"

Opoe turned to us. "When my sister died, I got all her clothes. She had fine stuff. Real solid. She wasn't built like me, but it doesn't make any difference for an old woman. I've got a lot more from her that I've never worn yet. Some beautiful Sunday aprons. I've even got enough for Dientje, but she's got modern ideas in her head. Wants to go to a store. Pooh!" Opoe looked disgusted.

Dientje pretended she hadn't heard. Sini and I were slowly eating our breakfast, which tasted good.

"That's true." Opoe didn't want to give up the subject yet. "Textile they call that junk they're selling. Name's fancy enough. Textile. In my days we said cloth. And, boy, that's what it was. This stuff doesn't last. Rips on you while you're wearing it. You think you've got something new. Ha, after a couple of years it's old."

I didn't dare look at Sini. She was probably sucking in her cheeks, too, trying not to laugh.

"Okay, Ma. Enough. Well, I'm going to work. A couple of days a week I take my horse and cart to the bleachworks in Boekelo, the next town over. Can't live off this farm. Maybe we could if Dientje wouldn't eat so much."

"Johan, what'll the girls think?" She started downstairs with him. "I'll get you some water, so you can wash up."

A pump handle squeaked. A few minutes later she came back, carefully carrying a bowl of water. "Must've been fancy at the Hanninks," Dientje said. "They got real faucets, don't they? At least that's what people say." She sat down on the bed. "If you girls knew how dangerous it is for us to have you. We've never done this before, but how could we say no to the Hanninks?"

I dipped my fingers in the bowl. The water felt icy.

"You always get awfully nervous over nothing," Opoe said.

"Nothing? We haven't even got a hiding place like the Hanninks. You don't know what's what," Dientje said disgustedly.

I slowly rubbed my fingers over my face.

"You'll see, they won't keep us here any longer than they have to," Sini said after Opoe and Dientje had gone. "Dientje is frightened. She can't wait till we go back." Sini was probably right.

But I answered: "Maybe she'll become less afraid, and fight with the Hanninks over us. 'No, Mrs. Hannink, *we* want to keep them.' "

Wouldn't that be something? It made us laugh and laugh. From downstairs Dientje called, "For God's sake, girls, be quiet."

We decided to see what else there was upstairs. We peeked into Opoe's room. She slept sitting up apparently—four pillows. Her room faced the front, too. We closed the door. Then there were the stairs which were partly covered with a red runner. The uncovered parts were painted green. We looked around. All the walls were painted that same color. They must like green.

The back bedroom was much bigger, and there were two windows. We each went to one. Blue sky, the kind that meant cold weather. I could see several separate buildings in the back. The one closest to the house seemed to be some sort of garage. A little beyond that was a small house that looked like a chicken coop. Next to it was a low, wide building.

"That must be the stable," Sini said. "I think I hear cows."

Across the path from the stable was a shed. Maybe that was where Johan kept his cart. Here and there, in between the buildings, were trees. Opoe came from the house with a pail in her hand. On one side her skirts were bunched against her leg. On the other side they billowed out. Windy day. Cold wind probably. She went into the chicken coop.

"Annie, let's go back, it's freezing in here."

Dientje was lighting the stove in our bedroom. Sini asked her whether she had any books.

"Books?" She stopped taking care of the stove. "What kind?"

"To read."

"Wait, I think Johan has one. Where does he keep it? I'll ask him tonight. We've got a Bible around the house. Did you mean that?"

"No." We laughed. We should have brought something to read from the Hanninks. Silly.

"I read, too, but not every day. Sometimes I look at the paper. But Johan, he reads every word of it. He remembers it, too. Me, I forget." With an embarrassed look at us, Dientje left the room.

We sat around the stove and spat on it. It made nice hissing sounds.

"O God, how much longer," Sini cried.

"Six days," I said. She hadn't heard.

"The war has got to be over by spring. Annie, do you think it will be?"

I was getting tired of that question. She asked it all the time, and how was I to know.

I was pleased to see Opoe come in. "I thought I'd darn these socks here, talk a little bit to you. Poor things, being inside all day." She sat down heavily.

"Fui-fui, God-o-god-o-god, what a human being doesn't have to go through!"

"Opoe," Sini and I cried at the same time, "are you sick?"

"Why?"

"Because of what you said."

"What did I say? I don't remember. No, I'm not sick. Not yet. It'll come. Now, let's see." Opoe stuck one hand in a black sock. Several knuckles showed through the hole. "That Johan. Such big holes." She pulled her hand out again, unrolled some wool from a skein, took a needle from several that were stuck on her apron, held the yarn in her right hand, needle in her left, pushed her glasses down toward the tip of her nose. She held the needle up against the light. Her right hand trembled on its way to it. She missed.

"Let me do it for you, Opoe."

"No, no." She tried again.

"Come, give it to me." Sini got up and took the needle and yarn from her.

"I'm becoming helpless. Old. Bah. Thank you."

"Maybe you should go to an eye doctor."

"Nonsense. I'm wearing glasses already. I'm getting old. That's what happens. No, at my age it doesn't pay to go to an eye doctor. What can he say?"

She bent her head over the sock. Once in a while she wiped a tear from her cheek. They weren't crying tears. They were a different kind—straining-to-see tears.

"Want me to help you, Opoe?" Sini asked.

"No, your hands aren't used to this kind of work."

"I mean it, Opoe. I used to work on a farm. I even

know a little bit about sewing, and I have very strong hands."

"You worked on a farm?" Opoe sounded as if she didn't believe Sini.

"Yes. I have a milking diploma, too."

"Milking diploma? They give those? Not here in the country, they don't. We just do it. Milking diploma. God-o-god-o-god! That's too crazy. If I got a diploma for everything I know about a farm, I'd have a chest full. Planting-potatoes diploma, manure-spreading diploma, feeding-cattle diploma. How come you worked on a farm?"

"I liked the work."

Opoe had stopped moving her needle up and down in the hole. "Now, that's something."

Speechlessly Opoe handed Sini the other sock. She brushed a few wispy hairs back from her face. I noticed that the braid at the back of her head was brown, not white like the rest. It had been coiled around and around and was held together with lots of hairpins. How come Opoe has two-colored hair? I wondered.

Dientje came upstairs, carrying four cups and a pot. "We can all have some coffee up here. But one of us'll have to go downstairs soon, in case anybody comes in."

"Can't you lock the door?" I asked.

"During the day?" Opoe and Dientje laughed. "If somebody came to the house and couldn't get in, you know what would happen? An hour later all of Usselo'd know it. No, that we can't do."

Dientje rapidly drank her coffee. "Johan'll be home in an hour. That's when we eat dinner."

"Can't stand this coffee," Opoe complained after Dientje had left. She got up. "Fui-fui, God-o-god-o-god."

Johan walked in, smelling of winter weather. "Hi, girls, can you stand it? Pretty lazy life you're leading. Eh? Feel." He put his hands on my cheeks.

"Ooh, stop, Johan. They're freezing."

On his way out, he almost bumped into Dientje, who came in carrying a deep steaming bowl. She put two forks on the table and left.

"What's for dinner?" We looked. Potatoes, beans, and meat.

Sini speared a piece of meat on her fork and smelled it. "I thought so—pork. We'll have to leave it. Just eat the rest. I wonder when they'll bring us plates."

We waited and. waited. Soon steam stopped coming from the bowl.

"Sini, Dientje must have forgotten about the plates. Didn't you see in what a hurry she was? Can't we eat?"

"I guess you're right." She pushed the meat to one side, took her fork, and marked off a dividing line. "That's for you. This is for me."

We giggled, and chewed, painstakingly eating around the meat.

It was still there when Dientje came to take the bowl away. "Didn't you like the meat? Now, that's a pity." She looked unhappy.

"Dientje, we're Jews."

"Ja, I know."

"We're not supposed to eat pork. That's what it was, right?"

"Ja. But what did you eat at the Hanninks'?"

"We just didn't eat meat when they had pork."

"But that's all we ever eat. Once in a while a nice piece of veal, and chicken at Christmas, but for the rest, pork. And a couple of times a week, bacon. Mother, come upstairs. Something's the matter." Dientje's voice sounded nervous.

Opoe came. Dientje explained the situation to her. Together they bent over the bowl.

"Maybe they left the meat because it wasn't soft enough. I had trouble, too."

"No, Opoe, we never even tried it." Sini's face was blotched.

"But," Opoe said, "the potatoes and beans were fried in the same pot with the meat. Now, you ate those. So, you also ate pork, in a way."

Embarrassed, I looked at Sini. "You're right," she said, "tomorrow we'll try."

A few days went by. Every night Dientje reminded Johan that he'd have to ask Mr. Hannink when he was going to take us back. "I'm so afraid the Germans will get us, Johan. You heard what happened when they caught that Jew in Enschede."

"Ja, ja, woman. I know."

"He was taken away. But, Johan, the people who

hid'm were shot. If they catch us, Johan, that's it. That's it."

Johan said he'd talk to Mr. Hannink. "Don't worry, woman. I know."

He knew what? I didn't want to go back to the Hanninks'. And Sini didn't either. We liked farms. Farms were nice, cozy. Johan, don't ask. Don't listen to her. And if Dientje wants us to go, why did she tell me she was going to make me a dress out of an old one of hers? A pretty flowered one, too. Would she bring the dress over after it was finished? But I didn't want that; I wanted it here. Miserably I stared at my hands. They should have scratches on them, from playing. Why didn't they?

When Dientje nagged Johan again several days later, he became impatient with her. "Goddammit, woman, don't talk about it again."

"Dientje, don't bother him. He's worked hard today." That was Opoe. I smiled at her, but just a little bit.

The next day Dientje took my measurements for the dress. "It's going to look pretty on you," she said. "Come here and give Dientje a kiss."

Johan wasn't going to talk to Mr. Hannink, he said. "You girls are to stay right here."

I put my arms around his neck. "I like you, Johan."

"Ja, ja." He looked at Sini.

"Johan, you've got to feed the cows now," Dientje said nervously.

"You milk 'em first; then I'll come. Boy, have I worked today." He jumped up. "Damn, it's time to listen to the radio. Want to come with me tonight?"

Stealthily we followed him down the stairs. Before Johan let us go through the door that led into the good room, he went to the kitchen. He locked the door, and pulled down the shades there and in the good room. "C'mon."

In the room we turned left and went through another door. We were standing in a hall, which had three doors leading off it. Johan climbed on a chair. He pulled a wide plank out of the ceiling and stuck his hand in the opening. An old radio appeared. He pushed it to the edge of the hole, pulled down the cord, and plugged it in a socket near the floor. A voice from the radio whispered, "Here is Radio Oranje."

"That's it," Johan said. "Quiet."

Sini and Johan stood on their toes to hear better, their faces raised toward the hole. News, the real kind.

"Johan, did you ever find that book Dientje said you had?" I asked later in the evening.

"You wouldn't be interested. It's the farmer's almanac. We don't have real books in the house. We're just dumb peasants."

"Oh, Johan, you're not," Sini said.

He looked satisfied. "No, I guess not." He tipped his chair backward until it seemed about to fall, stuck out his legs, crossed his arms over his chest. "There are lots dumber. I'll tell you what we can do. We know

the minister pretty well. Every time I'm in his house
—when I've an errand there—I look my eyes out.
Books all over the walls. Walls. Can you picture that?
Dientje'll go to'm soon and borrow some. The Hanninks, of course, have books, but I don't want to go
there. If the Germans ever catch'm doing all those
things, they might want to find out who came to their
house a lot. Can't risk anything now with you girls.
Got to get you through the war. Yep."

Opoe was standing in the doorway. She was taking
hairpins out of her braid. With the last pin the braid
came off. That's just what I thought. Her own hair
ended in a thin wisp in the back. She put her nightcap
on. "Not that I'll sleep, but it's bedtime," she announced.

Shouldn't we have a hiding place for them, too?
Dientje asked. "Johan, don't be stubborn. Under the
bed's no good. Even the Hanninks had one for them."

I stared at Dientje with big eyes. Please not another
cave. I . . . I was afraid in it.

"I wouldn't have one of those," Johan said. "What
good is it to have a hiding place out in the yard. No,
that's not for me. I've just thought of one, woman,
that'll make you wonder why smart Mr. Hannink
didn't think of it."

After that, on the days that Johan didn't go to
Boekelo, he worked on the hiding place. He was going
to cut the closet in our room in half and put in shelves.
"Sini, hand me that piece. Good. Out of the way,

Annie. I know you're curious. Dientje, you're in my way, too. Move. That's the girl, Sini. Just right."

Dientje turned to Opoe. "I didn't like the way you washed the dishes this afternoon. There were still crusts in the pans. Next time a salesman comes by with a suitcase full of glasses tell'm to go some place else. You're not going to buy another pair from one of those men."

Why did Dientje yell at Opoe? Just because of a crust? She should yell at Johan. He was the one—telling her and me to get out of the way. But I guessed she didn't dare. What if he got mad? When the hiding place was ready, Johan called Opoe and Dientje and me. We had to look at the bottom shelf, he said. "There's nothing special about it," said Opoe. "It's got stuff on it just like the other shelves."

Johan looked triumphantly behind him. "Wait." He took the clothes off the shelf and put them next to him on the floor. Then he lifted out the shelf. With both hands he removed the piece of wood that was in back of it. A dark opening showed, the doorway to our hiding place.

"That Johan," Opoe said proudly.

"We'll keep it open from now on, so the girls can get right in. Then one of us'll put the door back, lower the shelf, straighten the clothes on it, and close the door. As simple as that." He picked the clothes off the floor and piled them in a corner of the shelf.

"But what do we do if they're by themselves? Who'll put the piece back and lower the shelf?" Dientje asked.

"I thought of that. One of us'll always be around the house. And most searches are held at night anyway. Now, girls, you show how well it works."

Sini went first. She stuck her head in, then her shoulders. The rest of her followed. She moved to the side and left the opening free for me. If Sini could do it, I could. This hiding place wasn't under the ground. No earth could fall on me. It was just inside a closet, a clothes closet. It even had some pretty material in it. Slowly I got in.

But this hiding place was pitch-dark, too. "Sini," I whispered. Where was she? I felt around with my hand for her. I didn't have to stick it out far.

"Can you sit sideways?" Johan called.

We tried. We just could, as long as our legs were alongside each other.

"Don't try sitting down facing the room," Johan called. "You'll get yourselves stuck. Okay, come out."

I went first. Boy, what a big room we had. And it was so light.

Every day we'd have to practice getting in and out, Johan said, until it took us no time. "Not a bad hiding place for a dumb farmer, eh?"

"No, Johan."

It got dark early. Real winter afternoons. Sometimes I could hear a car pass. The person in it must have been dressed for going out. In a coat. With a scarf, maybe. I put my hand on my throat. I used to wear a scarf in the winter. Where was it? Where? I clenched my fists.

What if I knew where the scarf was? What would I do with it? Tell me. What?

Darker. I stared at the stove. It gave off a red glow, the only point of light in the room. Once in a while a coal dropped. Thud.

6

GIRLS, is this what you meant?" Opoe walked in with a calendar in her hand.

We almost grabbed it from her. Yes, that's what we meant. The year 1943. Sini took a pencil and rapidly crossed off day after day. Most of January was gone—for good.

Opoe watched Sini with a puzzled expression on her face. "What are you doing, messing it up?"

"We're marking the days off."

"What's that supposed to do?"

"So we can see they've past."

Opoe eyed us suspiciously. "Well, that's new to me. Days go fast anyway. Take me. I'll be seventy-one on Sunday."

"This Sunday?"

"Yes, sure. Crossing off days. What's next?" She was still shaking her head when she went downstairs.

We had been living there for almost a month? But I didn't even know what the house looked like.

"Johan, do you have a picture of the house?"

"A what?" he said. "Why would I want a picture of it? I can see it every day. When you go through the gate, you come to a little garden where Opoe grows flowers—geraniums. That's right in front of a couple of rooms you haven't been in. I'll show them to you after the war. They look out on the street. In between those rooms is the front door. But nobody uses it. They go past the side of the house right into the kitchen."

"I know. That's where we came in, too."

The house was red brick with green trimmings, Johan told me. I tried to memorize what he had said. It was silly to live in a house and not know what it looked like.

We still had nothing to read either. And he had promised. . . . "Johan, when can Dientje go to the minister to borrow books?"

"Tomorrow," he said.

The next day I finished my math fast. It was a bore, a b-o-r-e. Why did Sini make me do a page every day? She wasn't my teacher. I scribbled an answer down. Fast. I'd have to be ready when Dientje came back, so that I could read.

Here she was. Jubilantly she opened her shopping bag. "A book. And look what a fat one. Are you glad?"

Yes. But there was only one. How come?

Sini took the book out of the bag. "*War and Peace*" she read. "Dientje, thank you. What did you tell him?"

81

"Well, when he opened the door, I said, 'Reverend, Johan's bored evenings.' 'Come in my study,' he said. 'Well, I said, you know my Johan's really a smart man.' 'I know,' he said. And then I had to come out with it. I said, 'Reverend, he wants to read a book.' 'Very well,' he said. 'Does he have a special one in mind?' 'Well, no,' I said. 'I don't want you to think that we don't want to go out and buy a book. But we don't go into Enschede too often these days, and I wouldn't know what to look for.' Then I started looking at those walls. 'How about that one?' I said, pointing at the fattest book. 'Fine,' he said, 'and I'd like to talk about it with Johan after he's read it.' Of course, that's the bad part about it. 'No rush,' he said, 'he can keep it all winter.' And then I did a smart thing, I think. I said, looking at the title, 'Reverend, a book with this title he'll read in a few weeks. Can I bring it back then and get another one?' 'Of course,' he said. 'Goodness, Johan must really be bored.' I had to put it in a bag, so nobody outside would see me with it." She chuckled. "Me coming out of there carrying a book."

All of a sudden she looked less elated. "I wish I could've brought you two books, but that would've made him suspicious."

"We can share it. You're wonderful, Dientje."

It was almost embarrassing to see how happy she was.

"Annie, this is really not a book for a ten-year-old," Sini said after Dientje had left.

"You forget, I'm almost eleven," I answered haughtily. She just said it because she didn't like sharing it. Well, I didn't either. "You think this is too grown-up for me? Ha, you don't even know what I've read." There. Let her worry.

But Sini laughed. "Okay," she said. "We'll take turns."

Sini settled in front of the stove with the book, her feet on the first rung of the chair, left hand under her head, little finger in her mouth. She bit it constantly. The skin would get red, raw.

"Sini," I said urgently.

"What?"

"Don't bite your finger. It'll start hurting."

A little while later, it was back in her mouth. I looked away, at the watch. I still had another half hour to wait before it was my turn. I picked up the poker and furiously drew designs on the linoleum with it.

In the middle of Sini's third turn, Johan came and said he was going to listen to the news. "C'mon, girls, get off your butts, or are you too busy now?"

Sini immediately closed the book. She had not been in such a hurry when I told her, her time was up! Sulkily I walked behind them.

I should have stayed upstairs. I could've gotten in ten extra minutes of reading. Why had I come? Johan and Sini were standing on a chair, their heads almost in the hole, near the radio. That's what Father was probably doing, too, if he had the chance. Nothing was any different from when I was six. Sini would never miss me. Look at that. Her head was practically on Johan's shoulder. Dientje would yell at Opoe if she saw them.

The chair started to squeak. They were dancing on it, their feet going up and down. "God almighty," Johan said in an excited voice. "Guess what, the Germans have lost in Russia, in Stalingrad. They're running around in circles, trying to get away from the Russians, but they can't, the guy said. Here, I'll let you listen, too."

He lifted me onto the chair. I pushed my ear against the radio. I didn't know it could say nice things, too!

"Is that so," Opoe said politely when she heard the news. "And they're running? Poor things."

"But, Ma, they're Germans."

"I know, I know. But they've got mothers," she said. We all laughed; Dientje, too. It was easy to laugh that night.

It was, but not now. I couldn't sleep, so many planes were going over on their way to Germany to drop bombs. Even the daily newspapers mentioned it. A disgrace they called it. Disgrace. Pooh, Opoe would say.

I burrowed my head deeper in the pillow and stuck a finger in each ear. Ooh, what a horrible noise. Please don't drop bombs here. Please. They could, Johan said. Enschede had factories that made equipment for the German army, and the English and the Americans had bombed those in other Dutch towns.

Opoe came in. "As if I don't sleep poorly enough."

"I'm going to have someone build me an air-raid shelter," Johan yelled over all the noise. "I've got just the place for it, on the walk between the house and the stable."

"But what if the war's going to be over soon?" Dientje said.

"Eh, nonsense. I don't really think so. In the meantime we could all get killed here in bed."

After a while I stuck my head out from under the covers. The planes were flying higher now. The siren blew again. It was over.

"If Hendrik knew. God-o-god-o-god, what a person doesn't have to live through."

Who could Hendrik be?

Still I couldn't sleep. Sini was tossing and turning, too. I crawled out of bed. "What's the matter with you?" I whispered.

"Nothing."

"Yes there is."

"All right, there is. For a while tonight I thought I saw the end of the war. That's what's the matter with me. It's never going to be over, I know. I'll grow old here, and ugly."

Clumsily I patted her head. What if Sini were right? Noiselessly I got back into bed. Had there really been an eighty-year war?

Didn't we have to give Opoe something for her birthday? But what? "Dientje, would you go to Enschede for us and buy her something?"

Dientje laughed. There wasn't anything in the city that Opoe would like, she said. "But we're giving her some material that Johan's bringing home from the bleachworks. Maybe he can get another piece that you can give her."

What would she do with it, we asked.

"Nothing, of course," Dientje said wearily. "She only wears those things her sister left her."

That night in bed Johan whispered, "Let's all eat dinner together on Opoe's birthday."

"Johan, I can't carry everything upstairs."

"I didn't mean upstairs. We'll all eat downstairs."

"But, Johan, the girls."

"Them, too. We'll eat early, and we'll draw the shades."

"But, Johan, we never do that. Draw the shades during the day. And we always have company for her birthday. They could come any time."

"They don't. Nobody ever came before three. Okay, I'll tell you what. We won't draw the shades; we'll close the gate. That way we can hear if somebody's coming or not, and it'll give the girls enough time to go upstairs."

I snuggled deeper under the covers. Life was not as dull as Sini kept telling me. We did plenty of things. Now, take next Sunday, for example. We would eat downstairs, and not even after dark. Oh, no, during the day, just like everybody else.

Contentedly I closed my eyes. Birthdays were wonderful.

86

"Happy birthday, Opoe," we said on Sunday morning.

"Ja, ja, not so happy. Just a year older."

"But, Opoe, you don't look older."

"That doesn't mean a thing. It's how you feel."

"Are you going to get dressed up today?" I asked.

"Me? O-god-o-god-o-god, dressed up. What for? I haven't gotten dressed up for nineteen years. No, that time's gone."

Not for nineteen years? I looked at Sini's face. She seemed puzzled, too. It smelled good upstairs. Cooking smells. Johan had said he was going to kill one of their chickens. "If you hear one of 'em carrying on like crazy, that's the one."

And now it was eleven o'clock. I fidgeted back and forth on the chair. The kitchen must be all steamed up, from the cooking. You'd have to wipe off the window if you wanted to see out.

What was Sini doing, licking a finger and brushing it over her eyelashes? Up the top lid, down the lower lid. What did *she* need to get that dolled up for? It wasn't her birthday.

"Girls. Okay?" Johan called.

Sure, okay.

The table in the good room was set for five, with deep soup plates and spoons and forks. They were pretty plates, too, and there was one for each of us.

"You're surprised, eh? You didn't think a farmer would have such fine things, right? I know. I can tell by your faces. Well, Ma, here's to you." Johan raised his soup spoon. "May you live to be a hundred." We lifted our spoons, too.

"Ja, ja, a hundred. I'll be lucky if I'm going to live for another year."

Slowly Opoe ate her chicken soup. "Not bad, Dientje. A little thin, though."

Dientje winked at us.

It was fun being downstairs and eating from a plate. Sini and I were sitting near the door that led upstairs. Just in case we had to run, we sat on the edge of our chairs. I looked around the room. On the big chest along the wall were several yellowed portraits, probably of relatives. On the wall opposite me hung an embroidered picture. In the middle was a brown horse, front leg raised. In each of the four corners there was a bird. Embroidered notes of music came from their bills. But how come the birds were so large? They were at least as big as the horse's head. Birds weren't that large? Were they a special kind?

"What're you staring at, Annie?" Opoe asked.

"That picture."

"You like it?"

"Yes," I said hesitantly.

"I made it myself about fifty years ago, when my eyes were still good."

"What kind of birds are they, Opoe?"

"Eh, just birds."

"Is it a special kind of horse?"

"No, just a colt." A colt?

"Very nice, Opoe," Sini said.

"Dientje, I'd like you to make me an apron out of the cloth the girls gave me. It's real nice."

"I'll use the piece we gave you last year. It's just like the new one you got from them. It's not good for all that material to lie around."

"No, I like this new piece better."

"But it's almost the same pattern as the piece you've already got. When I gave it to you last year, you made a face as if you didn't like it." Dientje's face was red. "You just don't like anything I do around here anymore." She nervously finished her soup. "Girls, don't leave anything on your plate. I'm going to put the rest of your dinner on it. Johan, don't just sit there. Can't you help me bring in the pans?"

"What, you want me to do everything around here?" But he got up and followed her into the kitchen. He came back with a big black pan.

"Johan, don't put the pan on the table till I've spread that newspaper over it." Dientje's voice was edgy. She turned to Opoe. "What would you like. A leg or what?"

"Give me something that's easy to chew. A piece of breast maybe."

Dientje put chicken, string beans, and potatoes on everybody's plate. With a soup ladle she put brown gravy over the food. For a while nobody said anything. We ate. Johan kept one hand on his hip and crammed forkfuls of food into his mouth. So did Dientje. Only she stopped once in a while to nod at us. "C'mon girls, you're so thin. Eat up."

Opoe had trouble chewing. No wonder. She only had a couple of teeth. How could she eat? With her gums? Stealthily I watched her. She picked up her piece of chicken, stuck it into her mouth, closed her lips over it, and pulled. The piece she held in her hand now was a little bit smaller than before. She chewed and chewed. I was afraid she'd catch me looking at her. I quickly turned my eyes away.

"Mother, you should eat your beans, too. They're good for you. They've got vitamins in them, or what d'you call them," Dientje said. "Isn't it so, girls?"

Sini nodded.

"Pooh, vitamins. What are they? Those beans are hard."

"Opoe," I asked, "why don't you get false teeth? A lot of people have them."

Sini stepped on my foot. Ow. What did she do that for? Maybe Opoe had never thought of getting false teeth.

"At my age? That doesn't make any sense. I've been chewing like this for a couple of years now. It'll be all right for as long as I'm going to be around. False teeth. Hendrik should know. Want to feel how hard my gums are? Just like teeth. Here, give me your hand."

I shook my head. "No, Opoe, I can see."

"Nice chicken, Dientje," Johan said. "I hadn't thought she'd be this tender. After all, she was no youngster. How long had we had her?"

"Couple of years, I think. No, maybe longer."

"She was a snippy one," Opoe added. "Every time

I'd come in to feed them, she'd be right there pushing the others away. I won't miss her."

We all chewed. "Very good, Dientje," Sini said. Dientje beamed with pleasure.

"Yes, she can cook good," Johan said. "She looks it, too. Don't you, wife?"

"Oh, Johan. Mother, why are you leaving all that chicken on your plate? It's so good."

"It's too tough."

"But that's not true. The meat is so tender you could suck it. Look."

"That's what I tried. Now don't feel bad about it. I know you meant well. Is there any dessert?"

"I made that pudding you like."

"I hope you let it get cold enough."

Opoe lifted her apron up to her face and wiped her mouth with it. Dientje did the same with hers. Johan carefully stuck two fingers in his pocket and pulled out a large red handkerchief. After he had wiped his hands and face on it, he passed it on to me. I turned it around until I found a dry part, then passed it on to Sini. She didn't even look for an unused corner.

"You wouldn't think food was rationed," Johan said, "when you look at us. In the cities people haven't got it so easy. Those food coupons don't buy much. Just enough so that you're always hungry. I bet your father isn't getting very much to eat near Rotterdam. What's Mr. Hemmes again? A retired bookkeeper? Boy, I hope somebody's giving them food coupons for your father. Otherwise they're really in trouble. No, I'm glad I'm a farmer. I always say, drowning a fish and starving a farmer, that's not easy."

We laughed, Johan loudest of all.

"I wish you could stay down here this afternoon," Opoe said. "It sure would be nice."

"Maybe next year for your birthday, Ma, they can come from Winterswijk and spend the day with us."

"Johan, do you really think we might be free by then?" Sini asked anxiously.

"I got my doubts. The Russians are doing fine in Russia. I know. So are the Allies in North Africa. In Russia the Germans are killed in the snow; in Africa, in the hot deserts." Johan grinned. "Boy, the Italians must be mad. Here Hitler talked them into coming into the war with'm, and all they've gotten out of it is a mess. Lots of them are dead in Africa, too." He shook his head. "I don't know what to say. Damn."

Slowly we went back upstairs. Someone had opened the gate.

Opoe hadn't told us that the Hanninks would be there, too. They came upstairs to see us, as if *we* were giving the party. "Hi."

"You know what we brought Opoe?" Mrs. Hannink asked. "You'll never guess. Cologne."

We all laughed. Opoe would put the bottle away in some closet or throw it out. Bah, new-fangled junk, she would say. So funny. What did Mr. Hannink ask? Did we ever hear from Father and Rachel?

"You know," Sini said, "Rachel is staying with a minister about forty miles from here. Sometimes she writes to Johan. Father does, too. But the letters tell us very little so that if someone opens them, he won't learn anything. And Johan doesn't want them to write very often because the mailman never used to bring letters before. People might become suspicious."

Mr. Hannink nodded. "Johan is right. Well, we have to go back downstairs before anyone else comes. It's a pity you can't be there. Opoe sits on a straight chair the whole afternoon, hands folded in her lap. And everybody keeps telling her that she should sit in the easy chair. 'Pooh' is all she says, 'not me. I can take it easy soon enough, when I'm bedridden.' She has been saying this for years, and every year she looks better and younger."

"Was Hendrik her husband?" Sini asked.

"Yes," Mrs. Hannink said, but there was no more time to talk. The gate had opened again.

Sini and I sat near the stove, listening. How long would all that company stay? "Probably until milking time," Sini said.

My God, that was hours away.

Why were they laughing so much. At Opoe? We should go downstairs now as if it was the most normal thing in the world.

"Sini?" But Sini didn't even answer me. She was too busy staring at the wall. Oh, hello, everybody, we'd say. How are you? We decided to come, too. You seemed to be having such a good time. Yes, Dientje, we'd love some tea. Thank you. And nobody would look at us as if we were special. Special.

I bent over the stove and spat on the lid. I liked the noise it made.

"Poor Rachel," Sini said, "being all by herself."

It was getting dark, and the company was still in the good room, laughing. What was that? Was somebody coming up the stairs?

"Fui-fui, how tired can a person get!" Opoe came in. "It's nice and quiet up here," she whispered. "All that smoke downstairs. Bah. Spectacle every year. Well, not that many more years."

Opoe lifted her apron and stuck her hand into a pocket in her dress. "I brought you some cake. I had a good time sneaking a piece into my dress. It's not bad. Dientje baked it herself. Well, I've got to go back, sit on that chair some more."

"How much longer, Opoe?"

"Who knows with these people? They're apt to stay too long. Bah!"

Sighing, Opoe went back downstairs. Contentedly we bit off small pieces of the cake. What did Opoe mean by not bad? It was very good. The company would leave soon. They wouldn't stay all night.

It was getting cold in the room. Without making any noise, Sini took the lid off the stove. One by one I took coals out of the scuttle and plopped them into the stove. After the tenth coal Sini eased the lid back on. No sense putting in more, the day was almost over.

7

I STRAINED my ears. Clip-clop, clip-clop. What was that noise outside? The little Groothuis boy? Where was he? In front of his house? Clip-clop, clip-clop. Jumping rope? Did he jump as high as I used to? I looked at the window. I wanted to see, not just hear. I got up. I took one step, and then another one. Sini wasn't paying any attention. There. I had passed the safe side of the bed. Another two steps, and I'd be able to see him. Clip-clop. He must be jumping high, because he came down hard.

"Annie, have you lost your mind? Come back."

I did, startled. "Why did you yell at me? You scared me."

Had I forgotten, Sini asked, what would happen if somebody saw me?

No, no, I hadn't. But what was so terrible about Poland? I stood in front of Sini. "Tell me, how often could they beat you?"

"Very often," she said.

"I wouldn't care. Really. Sini, you hear that?"

I stamped my foot. From downstairs Dientje called, "For God's sake, girls, be quiet."

He probably couldn't jump as high as Frits could. Frits who?

"Who did this? What an awful thing to do. In all my life I haven't been this mad." Opoe stormed into our room. Furiously she looked from Sini to me. "Come with me. I want to show you something, something terrible."

We followed her to the back bedroom. "But, Opoe, we're not allowed in there as long as the man's building the air-raid shelter."

"He's not here this afternoon." She pushed us inside. "I want you to look at this." The bottom drawer of the chest was open. *War and Peace* was lying in it. So? Dientje was going to take it back in a day or two.

"Who put that book there?"

"I did, Opoe," I said.

"Look what you put it on. Don't you have eyes? The only thing I still have left of my mother's."

I looked. Underneath the book was a lace cap. Part of it was pleated. "You mean that, Opoe?"

"Yes, that. What else? That cap. Never has anybody done anything like this to me before."

"But, Opoe, I didn't know."

"What's there to know? Couldn't you see? I don't know if I can ever forgive you."

"Opoe, I'm sure she didn't mean to," Sini said.

Opoe didn't seem to hear. She bent down and took the book off the cap. With a disgusted look on her face, she pushed the book into my hands. "Here. Such a heavy book it had to be, too."

"Opoe, I'm sorry." I had trouble keeping the tears out of my voice. What a miserable day.

"I don't care. You've ruined my cap." Opoe seemed to have trouble with her voice, too.

"What's going on?" Dientje started talking as she came up the stairs.

"That little one put the book you got for them on top of my cap. Why didn't she look where she put it? Now it's ruined."

"Come, show me. Maybe we can fix it."

The cap wasn't broken or anything. What was wrong with it? "I told Opoe I was sorry."

"I know you didn't mean to. Now, let's see." Dientje pushed at it, smoothed it. "I'll press the pleats. Then it'll look all right. You really didn't have to make such a fuss. My God, you've had that thing for so long. Mother, can't you see she's sorry? Give her a kiss, Annie, and she won't be angry anymore."

Hesitantly I approached Opoe. But she walked away.

"Anybody home? *Hoo-oo,* I'm coming upstairs. It's me."

Dini Hannink had come to see us? But why today? Opoe was angry. I was miserable. What did Dini want? She had come to warn us, she said. "The Germans are planning a house-to-house search tonight. They're looking for an underground worker who they think is hiding somewhere in Usselo."

The man had broken into an office in Enschede where food coupons were kept, Dini explained. He was going to distribute them to people who were hiding Jews, but somebody had betrayed him. Abruptly she left. There was someone else she had to warn. What would we have to do now?

"I wish Johan was home," Dientje complained.

"What a situation," Opoe said. "Let's have an early supper."

"What's that got to do with it?" Dientje's voice cracked. "Where's Johan? I don't want the soldiers to come when he isn't home. I'm scared."

"What d'you mean, where's Johan? It's Thursday. He's in Boekelo, of course. Dientje, keep your wits together. Just because Dini. . . ."

Sini and I went to our own room. It was not dark yet and wouldn't be for another hour. Now Dientje was angry, too.

When Johan came home, he said, "Don't worry about the search. That's nothing. Now we'll show the Germans what a fine hiding place you've got."

But we'd have to spend the night in it, he said, so that Sini's mattress wouldn't be around. They might rush in without warning.

"Johan, the girls will choke in that place. All night. What's the matter with you?" Opoe sounded angry.

"Ma, we won't close it up. We'll have enough time

to put the board in and arrange all the stuff on the shelf."

"But, Johan, they can't stand up all night."

"Ma, they can sit down. For one night they'll be all right."

"What if they don't find the person they're looking for?" Sini asked.

Johan scratched his head.

Then what? Would we never go to bed again?

"Tomorrow night we'll all go to sleep. Regardless."

"But, Johan," Dientje protested.

"I'm already such a poor sleeper," Opoe said from her chair, "and with this I might just as well not bother going to bed."

"Nonsense, Ma, you always say you can't sleep, but, boy, do you snore! You can't tell me you snore sitting up awake."

"I don't snore, either. Do I, Dientje?"

"Johan's right."

"Girls, did you ever hear me?"

I didn't dare say anything. What if she got angry again?

"It's hard to tell, Opoe, with all those airplanes flying overhead at night. Maybe that's what Johan and Dientje have you mixed up with." That was clever of Sini. Opoe looked pleased.

"They may not start the search until early morning," Johan said, "when they figure everybody's asleep. I sure hope they won't find the girls. Hey, Dientje." He nudged her with his elbow. "Look at Ma."

Opoe was sitting up straight with her arms folded

across her stomach, but her head was wobbling. Slowly it sank down until her chin touched her apron. There it stayed for a second. Then her head moved sideways, all the way over to her shoulder. A drop of spittle slowly moved to the corner of her half-open mouth. Would it slide down the side of her chin? No, she sucked it in. Her head jerked up, stayed up for a moment, and started the trip again. Funny, it moved back to the same shoulder.

"Eh, what did you say, Johan?"

"Nothing, Ma. I thought you never slept."

"I don't."

"Can't kid us. You've got four witnesses."

"Johan, I think maybe we should all go to bed. It's after ten," Dientje said. "Mother, you go, too."

With difficulty Opoe got up from her chair. "Johan, don't forget to leave the closet door open. We can't have them die on us."

"Oh, Mother." Dientje seemed annoyed. "They'll be all right. You're always worrying about the girls as if Johan and I don't know what's what."

"Now, if somebody knocks on the door tonight, I'll go down and let him in," Johan said, "after Dientje and I close up your hiding place. All you girls have to do then is to be dead quiet. If they open the closet and look around in it, don't move. If they knock on the walls to see if there's a space behind them, don't move."

We got in. Johan crouched in front of the closet. "If you need anything call us. You hear? Don't worry about a thing. You hear?"

Dientje stuck her hand inside the hole. "That feels like Annie's leg. Right? Where's your hand?" She put two round cold things in it—apples. "That's for when you get hungry. They're the kind you girls like."

We stood and sat. And stood and sat. "Sini, I'm so tired." I leaned against her. I shouldn't fall asleep, she said. But it was night, and very dark. Why shouldn't I sleep? "When are they coming, Sini?"

She didn't know, she said. Maybe they had already found the person they were looking for, in which case they wouldn't come at all. I might be here all night for nothing? "But, Sini . . ."

"Can you say the alphabet backward?" she asked. Animatedly I started reciting. I had never known how hard it was. It would take a long time to do it right.

"Girls, I'm so worried about you." Opoe's voice came from right in front of the hiding place. "Can you really breathe in there? Poor things. Can I get you something?"

"Maybe something to drink, Opoe."

"I'll go downstairs and make you some tea."

"N . . . m . . . l . . . k." Maybe by the time I got to a, she'd be back. I hurried.

"Here, stick your hand out. Careful, it's hot. Whose hand is that? Sini's?"

"What time is it, Opoe?" I asked.

"Little after two. Can you hear the planes in there?"

"Yes." I took another sip. "Are you still mad at me?"

"Eh? Mad? No. I can't understand how Johan and

101

Dientje can sleep through all this noise. You feel better?"

"Much, Opoe." I smiled in the dark.

We handed her the empty mugs. "Opoe, you're wonderful," Sini said.

"So what good does that do me?" Opoe answered. She moaned and groaned as she got to her feet.

Now she was going back to bed. She was going to stretch out her legs and lean against a pillow. Bed. The hot tea had made me even sleepier. "Sini, let me sleep."

"No." She pulled me to my feet, pinched me. "You've got to stay awake. Annie, I'll never be able to wake you up if they come. Wait, I'll teach you a little English. Then, when you go back to school, you'll be the only one who knows some. Give me your hand: *h-a-n-d*, hand. These five things are fingers: *f-i-n-g-e-r-s*, fingers."

"How do you say *doodmoe* in English, Sini?"

"Dead tired."

The night was over, and the soldiers had not come. With stiff sore legs we stumbled over to the bed. Sini took a mirror out of her pocket. I had never seen her face that white. After a fast look at herself, she put the mirror down. Slowly her fingers traced over her eyelids. They were puffed. Then she turned and buried her head in the pillow.

I picked up the mirror. Was that me? Couldn't be. I put the mirror under my pillow, away from Sini. I stroked the sheet. Bed.

It wasn't fair. Why had Johan asked only Sini to come to the stable with him tonight? Just because she knew something about cows? So what? I hadn't enjoyed sitting in that closet, either. Was she so special? Dientje didn't think so.

"Annie, don't spoil my good mood." Sini looked at me pleadingly.

Why shouldn't I? I wanted to walk to the stable, too, and back. Even back. I picked up the book I had been reading, the same *War and Peace* book. When was someone going to take it back and get another one? I opened it anyway, brooding. I wasn't going to do any math today. That would spoil her mood all right. My heart was beating furiously. I had been right. Her face was already red.

"Put that book away."

I didn't move.

"I'm asking you for the last time. Put it away."

I didn't move. I only swallowed nervously. Sini grabbed the book from me. "Give it back," I said.

"No. Do your lesson first."

"Give it back." I hunted for the right words. "If you don't, I won't speak to you for the rest of the day." There. I felt better already.

Maybe I had made a mistake when I said I wouldn't talk to Sini all day. It had happened so early. If I had just said for the morning only. No, I had to be reckless.

Oh, well, Sini didn't like it either. She probably had a headache. I looked at her. Sure she did. And did it show. Poor thing. She might not even be able to enjoy her outing tonight. Too bad.

I should've remembered how long days were, though. But she had forced me to do something that drastic. Nobody could push me around and not get punished.

We went to bed without saying good night. Well, at least today was over! But why didn't Sini say anything? Could I just start talking tomorrow morning? What if we didn't speak for another whole day? I lifted my head off the pillow. Was that someone crying? It must be Sini. Was she sorry? She should be, pulling my book away, going out.

I was sick of having lessons all the time. Just because she enjoyed teaching me shouldn't mean that I had to be her pupil every day. Why didn't she get somebody else? I wished she'd stop crying, though.

Noiselessly I sat up and looked over the edge of the bed. It was her all right. Her shoulders were shaking. Maybe I should say good night. I could do it very fast. If it would make her stop. . . .

Carefully I climbed out of bed. I shouldn't think too long about it. "Sini?" I whispered. She sat up and stuck out her arms.

Funny. I cried, too. Sini was right. What if the Germans had come to the house in the night and found us? They would have taken us away. Sini said they might have separated us, sent us to different concentration camps in different countries. We might never have seen each other again. We couldn't have told each other how miserable we had been not talking to each other all day. Then what?

Something was wrong with my legs, Sini said.

I looked at them. What?

"You wobble when you walk," Sini said in an alarmed voice. "Or are you doing it on purpose."

"No, of course not." Wobble?

"Now stand still and straighten your legs. They're crooked, Annie."

"Sini, they're not." They were? How did they get that way?

"Why didn't I notice it before. You don't move around enough. No wonder. Muscles need to be exercised." Anxiously Sini watched me. After the war my legs could be massaged, she said, but in the meantime I'd have to walk up and down the room. "One hundred times a day."

"No, Sini, not that many times." *My* muscles needed to be exercised. What about *hers?*

"Oh, yes. I'll count. One—two—three."

"What are you making Annie do, Sini?" Opoe asked. "Does she have to? Look at her. She doesn't like it."

"Opoe, if she doesn't exercise every day she'll get so stiff that she won't be able to walk anymore after the war."

"Oh, how could that be?"

"Don't say that, Opoe. It could."

"Stop for a minute, Annie, and drink your coffee."

"That's another thing that annoys me, Opoe. I don't want her to drink coffee any longer."

"My goodness, you're difficult today. Boy, o boy!" At the door Opoe turned around. "Maybe she can't have any more tea either, eh?"

"I don't want to walk anymore, Sini."

"I wish they wouldn't interfere," Sini said furiously.

I glanced at Sini. Would she get mad again because of what Dientje had just said? That I was going out tonight. Just me and Dientje. Sini and Johan could have their cows. Bah, smelly things. No, we were really going out. We'd have to take the bike to get there, to the farmer she used to work for. They were hiding ten Jews. That was a lot. One of them was a girl my age, Dientje said. I'd probably like her. Sure. Wasn't it nice of Mr. Hannink to have told Johan about them? What if the weather weren't good?

"Dientje, what if it's raining?"

"Don't worry, we'll go anyway."

What was I going to wear? Maybe the dress she had made for me. Maybe so. I should look nice, going on a visit.

"What's her name?"

"Whose name?"

"The girl's."

"I don't know. You're glad you're going out, aren't you?" Dientje beamed.

I nodded. "How long will we stay?"

"Not too long. Maybe an hour."

I'd better walk some more around the room. After all, I didn't want the girl to think I walked funny.

"You look fine," Sini said when it was time to leave. "You aren't going out without giving me a kiss?"

I was really getting too old for that kind of thing. Oh, well. I kissed her and walked down the stairs. At the bottom I looked up. I waved at Sini.

"You can come," Johan called softly.

Outside, Dientje was holding her bike. She wasn't going to turn the bicycle lamp on, she said. Then nobody would be able to recognize her.

I climbed on the back of her bike. Dientje put her right foot over the bar and pushed off. One, two pumps, then she sat down. "Put your arms around my middle. Hold on."

I knew we were going over a sandy road. Every once in a while the bike sank into a little hole. I could feel Dientje strain to get out of it. Was it a narrow road? Probably. Around Winterswijk all the side roads like this one were narrow. Were there any trees along the road? Carefully I stuck out my right arm. I didn't touch anything. My hands were cold. I put them inside Dientje's pockets.

"The path is getting very narrow here. Be sure to hang on."

Of course, I would. I didn't want to fall. I'd be all dirty.

The air smelled good. I opened my mouth wide.

Come in air, it's all right, it's me. Gratefully I rubbed my cheek against Dientje's coat.

"Evening." Dientje walked into the stable, holding my hand. "How've you been? This is Annie."

"I see, I see. Well, why don't we go talk to Mimi."

We followed the farmer into a room at the back of the stable. "Here's somebody to visit you," he announced.

The girl in the corner must be Mimi. She looked my age. From across the room we looked at each other.

"Go on, talk to her. That's why we came." Dientje pushed me in Mimi's direction.

How could I just talk to her? What would I say? I backed up and leaned against Dientje's chair. She was busy listening to the farmer and his wife.

"The baker must think something is going on here," he said. "Every day I come to the bakery with a large basket. Boy, you're eating well these days, he's already said to me more than once. Ja, I said, my kids sure have appetites. I get coupons from Mr. Hannink. How else could I get all that bread? I don't know where the baker thinks I get them from. I worry plenty over it."

Where did the ten people sleep? Did they have a hiding place? I looked around. Our room was cozier—just Sini and me. I wondered whether she missed me.

"Isn't she a little thing?" Dientje asked. "You should see her eat. Like a bird."

I wriggled uncomfortably.

"I don't know what's the matter with her tonight.

At home she isn't so bashful. You should hear her sometimes. C'mon, Annie, talk to what's her name? Mimi. She looks like a nice girl. Go on."

"Mimi, you're not shy. Talk to Annie," the farmer's wife said.

Mimi laughed sheepishly.

"Aren't you going to say anything to each other," Dientje wanted to know.

I felt my face getting red. I was sure that everybody was waiting to see whether we would start talking.

"Well, that wasn't a success," Dientje said a little while later. "Let's go home."

"Bye, Mimi," I said on my way out.

"Now, why didn't you start talking earlier? Is this the first thing you've said to each other?"

Ashamed, I nodded. It was silly. But what was there to say? I didn't even know her.

With a sigh of relief I climbed back on the bike. Once again I wrapped my arms around Dientje's middle. It sure did smell good outside. It was getting to be spring.

With spring my birthday came. I hadn't talked too much about it. That would have been childish. After all, I was going to be eleven. But from the moment I opened my eyes that morning I followed everybody's movements. They knew, didn't they? Yes, here came Johan with a package. "Annie, what d'you think of this," he asked.

"*Secrets of Nature*," I read, "by Gert von Natzmer."

"You didn't know, but I went to the city for it."

I leafed through the pages. "It looks like a fine book, Johan. Thank you."

"You have to give all of us a kiss," Johan said. "It's from all of us. You know, most of the books you see in the store have been written by Germans. I can tell from their names, even though I never had any German."

"Johan, Annie can't read any German," Dientje said. "What did you buy her a German book for?"

"Oh, c'mon woman, what d'you think I am. It's been translated."

"Could it be a good book," Opoe asked, "if it's written by a German?"

"Oh, Ma, what's that got to do with it? Boy, what a bunch of idiots in this house."

"I don't know. I was just asking."

I was looking at a picture of summer in Greenland. What a nice place!

But who had told Dini Hannink that it was my birthday? "You, Sini?"

Dini just laughed. The game of Monopoly she had given me was lying on the table. "Do you want me to play with you?" she asked.

"Yes, please."

"I'll play, too," Sini said. "How about you, Dientje?"

"Goodness, no. I'll just look."

Excitedly I watched Dini deal the money. Pretty, all the different colors. What a wonderful birthday I was having.

"Annie, don't you want to offer Dini anything?" Dientje asked.

Of course, I forgot. What a hostess! "Here, Dini, take a couple." I held the cookie jar in front of her.

"I'll tell you the damnedest thing," Johan said, "I bet you'll still be here for your next birthday. Yep, I think so."

"Why Johan?"

"Because the Germans won't leave unless the Allies come and drive them out. I can't understand why they don't land in Italy from Africa. All they have to do is cross a sea. Right? That's what I would do. Boy! An invasion of Europe, that's what we need. Then I can see the end after one more year. Not now. No."

I looked at Sini. The corners of her mouth were trembling. Why did Johan have to talk that way? How did he know we needed an invasion and that the end wouldn't come for another year? Couldn't it come, say, next week? How did he know? Well, maybe he was wrong. He could be. I'd tell Sini so later, after everybody was asleep. Johan didn't know everything.

Johan had left a newspaper on the table. "Burn it," he said, "after you've read it."

"Why, Johan?"

"Because this is a paper that's printed by underground workers, by people who want us to know what's really going on. Not like the goddamned official papers where every bit of news gets twisted around. But we're not supposed to know the truth. Those printers can get shot for what they're doing, and if the Germans find one of these things in the house, I can be arrested."

I picked up the newspaper. Don't give up hope, it said. The Germans *will* lose. It didn't say when. I guessed they didn't know either. I read a little further. No, what the paper said couldn't be true. It couldn't be. I had trouble going on, but I finished the article.

I put the paper down. Now I knew. Now I really knew what was in Germany and Austria and Poland. Murder camps. Sure I had known there were camps. That's where those trains took you. But I hadn't known that they were like this, that Hitler had told his soldiers to murder Jews, any time they felt like it.

They shoved as many people into the train as they could, with hardly any food or water. When the people arrived at the camps they were pulled out of the train. The old people, women, and children were taken away in cars. They turned around to wave at the others. The camps couldn't be so bad, not when the Germans picked you up in cars! They went to a special building. You can wash up here, they were told. You must be dirty after such a long trip. Lots of people went into the shower room holding pieces of soap in their hands, until the room was so full that the steel door could just barely be closed. No water was turned on. Gas was.

It didn't take more than fifteen minutes. Then they were burned. In ovens. Most of the time everybody was dead when this happened. Most of the time.

The young men were put to work. When they became too weak to work, their turn came, too. To go to the shower room.

Most of the people were Jews. But there were others, too.

Now I knew why I was here, why I shouldn't stand close to the window in the front room. I had just read why in a paper that told people what was really going on.

8

IT's warm enough now to do without the stove,"
Johan said. "I think I'll move you to the back room."

Anxiously I watched Johan. How would he be able
to get the table through the door? "Better be careful,
Johan."

"Don't worry, Johan'll do it. Easy enough."

Sini and I followed with the chairs. What else should
we bring? I walked back. Nothing, really. The calendar? It could stay. We'd be back every night. No, better
take it. I lifted the calendar off the thumbtack and
walked into the other room with it.

Now where would I put it? Here we wouldn't want
to look at it that often because we had windows. So a
corner would do. There.

I sat down by the window over the kitchen. Heavens,
the trees were all green. When had this happened?
Look at the sky. There was a lot of blue, but also
clouds. How fast could clouds go? Where did they

travel to? From the sky above one country to the sky above the next? So much to think about.

Where was Sini? I turned around. She was looking in the mirror. "Sini, I like it much better here. Don't you? Why don't you sit by your window? You want mine for a while?"

"Am I very pale?"

I studied her face seriously. "A little, but you don't look bad."

"But I look better with a tan, don't I?"

"Maybe. Your hair's nice again, though. Do you know why some clouds are dark, and others are white?" Sini didn't answer, and I repeated the question.

"No. Should I cut it again?"

"What?"

"My hair."

"I don't know. D'you think rain makes them dark?"

"I'm no longer as pretty as I used to be, am I? I know I'm not. I can see it myself. Tell me honestly."

I sighed. "To me you look all right."

"To you." Sini's voice sounded disgusted.

Now she wouldn't want to play Monopoly with me. I'd have to play by myself.

So much money for me. So much for her. Her? I could make it a him. No. Now, let's see. I'd better start. Wasn't that a foolish move she made. No wonder my pile of money was growing. Stupid. No, not me. You. You have to look out in this game. Yep. Thank you. Was that the last of your money? Well, that's what happens. You played poorly. I'll have to see whether you can play with me again. I'm not sure. It all depends.

I put the game away. What could I do next? Let's see. I could pretend Johan had asked me to come to the bleachworks with him. I closed my eyes, so that I could see better what he had told me about it. First we went to get the horse from the meadow. He put him in front of the cart. Johan climbed next to me on the cart, took his whip, clacked it, and off he went to Boekelo. We turned right, after we went through the gate.

"C'mon horse, move. The goddamn work is waiting."

And the horse ran. We entered Boekelo without having left Usselo, it seemed. Before a cluster of buildings, Johan stopped. He jumped off the cart and helped me down. "Here I am," he said to the man who came out of one of the buildings.

"Hey, Johan, fine fighting going on in Africa, right. Ja, ja, those Allies are something," he whispered.

Johan listened intently, nodding his head. Then the man opened the door of the building and started handing Johan bolts of cloth. Johan carried them over to the cart, one by one. Once in a while the horse impatiently pawed the pavement. When the cart was full, Johan took the reins again. "C'mon, move." The man went back inside.

In front of another building Johan stopped again. The door opened and a different man appeared. Johan carried the bolts of cloth over to him, one by one. When the cart was empty, we went back to the first building for more.

"On the cart, off the cart, Annie. It's the goddamnedest way to earn money. You're lucky not to have to work."

"Yes, Johan."

I opened my eyes. The palms of my hands were up, too, just like Johan's had been when he carried all that cloth.

I pushed my chair closer to the window. There Opoe was walking toward the chickens. She had already fed them once today. What was she doing this time? They didn't own her. Why were they so demanding? And Opoe just went. Sure, they were running after her. They knew why she had come again—food. Look at them. Choke on it. Go ahead. I say so.

What was Sini doing? She already had two cuts on her little finger from biting it. "Sini, take your finger out of your mouth."

Opoe was on her way back to the house. I waved. "Hi, Opoe." Nonsense, she couldn't hear me. But she saw me and smiled.

Look at those three chickens together, walking away from the group. They'd better not go to the vegetable garden. Opoe would yell at them.

It didn't turn dark till late. Some evenings Johan didn't even come home to listen to the news. He was too busy out in the fields. It made Sini both quiet and noisy. For hours she said nothing. Then all of a sudden, she cried, "Annie, how will we ever find out when the war's over if we don't listen to the radio? The papers won't tell us. We'll just sit here all our lives. I can't stand it any longer. Let me out!" She ran around the room, shaking her fists at the window. "Goddamn everybody! Tomorrow I want him home!"

Yes, out! "Me too, Sini." I'd run through meadows until my throat ached from breathing. But could I? I still wobbled, Sini said. That was when I walked though. Running might be easier. Yes, me, too.

I looked outside. How come I didn't get as angry as Sini? Wasn't I angry now? Sure.

Sini told Johan she wanted to hear the news again, and it was a good thing she did. The English and the Americans had landed in Sicily, and she and Johan were able to hear about it, firsthand.

"Didn't I tell you, eh? They crossed that sea, didn't they? Eh? How's that for a dumb farmer?"

"You knew it, Johan," Sini and I said.

"Get up. Dance with me."

Dance? Me? "Not so fast, Sini. Ow, ow, stop!"

"Little sister, this is the beginning of the end. Johan says so, too. Maybe a couple of more months. You know how close Sicily is to Holland, Annie?"

"No."

"Very close. Much closer to us than Russia and Africa."

Well, then we would certainly be home before the end of the year.

Sini was brushing her hair. Intently she studied her face in the mirror. "I'll be all right, I think. I look better already."

She did. Much.

What a lovely day! Just smell the air. Great! And doing my exercises wasn't that bad either. After all, I wouldn't have to do them for much longer. Sini even offered to play Monopoly with me. It was fun to lose again. I never did when I played with "her."

But what was taking the Allies so long, so terribly long? Maybe they didn't care when the war ended. They weren't sitting in a room all day. Like us.

Another day of rain. Hadn't we had enough of them? Gloomily I stared out the window. I hardly heard the Oostervelds come in.

"Mussolini is in jail!" Johan almost shouted.

"He is?" How could Sini's face change that fast?

"What was the matter with him?"

"Oh, Ma, you know. That goddamned clown. That Italian dictator. Hitler's best friend, the one who went into the war with him."

"Don't you know who he is, Mother?" Dientje asked. "How could you not know?"

"Ja, ja. Who put him in jail?"

"His Italian Fascist friends, who were tired of seeing their army lose all the time."

"O God-o-god-o-god, what friends!"

"That's right, Ma. Hitler must be furious. Boy, this is good news!"

Sure, it was. Very good news when it happened.

So was the fact that six weeks later the English had

landed in southern Italy. Still, what difference did it make? *N-o-n-e!* Even Mussolini was out of jail again.

It was fall, fall 1943. I followed a few leaves on their trip down. How long would it take for the trees to become bare? A month? Two months? It would be interesting to see. Maybe I should make some notes. I went to the commode to get pencil and paper. I listed all the trees. Then I entered the loss of the first two leaves.

Soon it became too cold to stay in the back room. "I'll move you girls," Johan said.

I stood up. Would we be back here next summer? That wasn't possible, was it? I wiped my face on my sleeve. Sini had better not see me. It would make her look even sadder.

I knew exactly where I was going to hang the calendar in our winter room: right there where I had left the thumbtack. I put my chair back by the stove.

Dini Hannink came to tell us that Miss Kleinhoonte was going to visit us. "She called Father and said that she would be here on Friday."

"Eh, who is she, girls?" Opoe asked.

"Mother, don't you remember? She's the high school teacher from Winterswijk they've told us about."

"A high school teacher? Coming here? God-o-god-o-god, what's next!"

Dientje's face was getting blotchy. "We've never had such fancy company. Is she coming on the bus?"

"No, on the bike, so she won't be noticed."

"How long will she stay?" Dientje asked. "Not that it makes any difference, or anything. I only have to know if she's going to be eating dinner here."

"What's the matter with you, Dientje? Somebody's coming on the bike all the way from Winterswijk and you're asking if she'll eat here."

"Well," Dini said, "I'll leave you, so you can talk some more about it."

"Dientje, what are you going to fix for dinner when she's here," Opoe asked. "Shall we kill that chicken?"

"Which one."

"The one that's forever laying her eggs in odd places."

"I'll ask Johan."

They both left, busily talking about the visit. Halfway down the stairs Dientje turned around. "Friday, she said?"

"Yes."

"That gives us a few days to get used to the idea." She sighed with relief. "Me, I've never even been to a high school."

Would Miss Kleinhoonte eat up here with us? What if we had the chicken? Would we all take it in our hands? From the same dish? No, Miss Kleinhoonte, you take that piece if you want to. I only touched it once. That would show her that I still had good table manners.

"What time is she going to come on Friday?" I asked.

"I don't know, Dini didn't say." Sini looked dismayed. "Well, probably not till eleven or so."

"Sini, I'm so excited."

"How do you think I feel? You never had her for a teacher. I did."

Just one more day. And the weather didn't look bad either. A couple of times a day Sini and I went to the windows in the back room to check on the sky.

At nine o'clock on Friday morning, I started to clean. Obviously I didn't have to do exercises today. I whistled. It was fun to dust. I should do it more often. Carefully I moved a cloth-covered finger over the wooden parts of the chairs. No wonder Sini asked me to dust. She knew I'd do a good job.

"D'you think I look all right?" Dientje walked in. Her face looked flushed.

"Dientje, you look beautiful. Can you walk in them?" I asked, pointing at her shoes.

"You didn't know I had such city things, did you? Yes, but I'm going to take them off when she's up here with you. Now, I think I'll bring you coffee and cookies when she first comes. Does that sound all right?"

"Sounds great, Dientje." She beamed with pleasure.

I picked a piece of lint off my dress. I looked pretty, too.

The door to the stairs opened. "Would you follow me, Miss Kleinhoonte. They're upstairs." Dientje sounded nervous.

Miss Kleinhoonte was just as frail as I remembered her. She hugged us. Sini's face was bright red. Mine probably was, too.

We each sat on a side of Miss Kleinhoonte, listening. An NSB-er had moved into our house, she said. And did we know that Rachel had left Winterswijk just in time?

"No."

"Well, a few hours after she left, the Germans came to your house to take her away."

Why hadn't Rachel come to the Hanninks'? we asked.

"Reverend Zwaal knew of a place where she'd be all by herself, and I think she decided it would be safer for all of you."

We said nothing for a while. I bent toward the stove. Saliva was gathering between my front teeth. "Annie," Sini warned.

Nervously I licked my lips. That was just in time. Another second and I would have let go.

"I brought you some textbooks for fifth grade."

I nodded. Fifth grade? That's what I was in now?

Uncertainly Dientje walked in, holding the cookie jar. "Here, Miss Kleinhoonte, I baked them myself."

"Thank you. I can see that you're taking very good care of the girls."

"We're glad we've got them," Dientje answered. "That sounds funny, doesn't it? Because, you know, if there wasn't a war, they wouldn't be here. I'm sure they can't wait to go back to Winterswijk. But we like the girls. We really do. We don't like the war, of course." Dientje stopped. She seemed confused. "And here the old mother's crazy about them. That little one can't do any wrong in her eyes. Except for that one time."

"What was that?" Miss Kleinhoonte asked.

Dientje told her about Opoe's cap. I fidgeted on the chair. Did she have to? I sighed with relief when she left.

What now? I had to stand up? Why?

"You know, Sini," Miss Kleinhoonte said, "Annie's very small for her age. I don't think she has grown at all. Do you make her exercise?"

"Oh, yes, every day. But she's always resisting me."

"Annie, Annie."

Even my ears felt red. Why did Sini have to tell on me? She could've just said yes. No, she had to put me on the spot. Wasn't I ever allowed to have a good time?

Ah, there was Opoe with our dinner.

"How does she like it here?" Opoe asked us.

"Very much," Miss Kleinhoonte answered.

"She should eat. She's had a hard day. On the bike. Fui-fui."

"I certainly will. It smells delicious. Where did you get chicken?"

"We've got 'em ourselves."

"Of course. You know, Sini and Annie told me your age. I can't believe that you're seventy-one."

"Almost seventy-two." For the first time Opoe looked at Miss Kleinhoonte. "And I feel every year of it. I've got aches and pains all over. How old are you exactly?"

"Just a few years younger."

124

"Boy, o boy, you don't look it, with those light clothes. The only thing is you shouldn't be so thin. That's not good for you. You'll be too weak when you get sick."

We were eating silently. The only sound was that of our forks on the plates. My face was getting warm again. Shouldn't we be talking? Why wasn't Miss Kleinhoonte saying something? I looked at her. She was busy chewing a piece of chicken. I hadn't noticed her eat before.

What a funny way she had of chewing! I couldn't take my eyes off her face. It made her look like a rabbit. Stop staring. What if she sees you? I felt a giggle come up. I swallowed desperately. The last thing I wanted to do was laugh. I turned my head away. Thank God, she had started to talk to Sini. But there, she took another bite. What a way to chew. I bit the insides of my cheeks. Don't laugh. No. No. But just like a rabbit.

Was that me, giggling? Yes. Stop Annie, or something awful's going to happen. Can't you stop? I giggled louder and louder. Hysterically. And I wasn't even having fun. What was the matter with me?

"Annie, what are you doing?" Sini asked nervously.

What did she mean, what was I doing? Giggling, of course. She couldn't want me to tell her why? Because the guest reminded me of a rabbit? I no longer giggled. I laughed. Sini glared at me. She got up and pointed a finger at me.

"Leave her," Miss Kleinhoonte said.

"No, I won't either. Annie, leave the table. Hurry up."

I got off the chair. Where should I go? It was cold in the other room. She wouldn't want me to go in there. My face was burning. With a bent head I shuffled over to the corner by the door. I sat down with my back to them. I started to cry. What now? Don't, please. I liked Miss Kleinhoonte, too. It wasn't easy to sob and make no sound, stay perfectly still. I hurt all over.

"You're sure you don't want to sleep here?" Dientje asked Miss Kleinhoonte.

"No, thank you. I'm going back."

"Forty miles a day is an awful lot at your age," Opoe warned. "I don't see how you can do it, being so thin. Can't you at least stay for supper?"

"No, I have to leave."

"I'll pack up some food for you," Opoe said.

"Good-bye Miss Kleinhoonte. Thank you for the books." Hesitantly I stuck out my hand. Would she take it after the way I had behaved?

She kissed me. I was sorry I would never have her for a teacher.

Funny that having company should make you tired. So Mother was buried in the Jewish cemetery. That was near home. We should be happy that she died when she did, Miss Kleinhoonte had said. A week later the Germans came to the hospital to take all the Jewish patients away.

I felt I would cry again. Why had they done that? I dug my nails in my hands. No. What was the matter with me today? But why?

I climbed into bed. Dientje lifted her hand and pulled the light cord. At least nobody could see my face anymore. Just in case. . . .

It was almost the fifth of December, and Sini and I started to make up rhymes for everybody. Without them, it wouldn't seem like Saint Nicholas Day. When it was Opoe's turn to read hers out loud, she lifted the piece of paper solemnly, bringing it close to her eyes.

> Boy, o boy, am I tired
> But still I can't go to sleep.
> What can be the matter with me?
> It must be that I'm getting old,
> I'm sure that's what it is.
> Seventy-two less thirty-nine days,
> That's very, very, very, very old.

"Aren't you ashamed of yourselves, making a fool of an old woman?" But Opoe didn't sound angry. "Fui-fui, I haven't laughed like this for years. Hendrik should hear."

"Eh, Ma, don't you think the girls are pretty fresh to tell you this?"

"Ja, ja, they are." Opoe laughed. "Let's have another drop of coffee. Dientje, that applecake you made isn't bad. But why didn't you put more apples in it? We've got 'em in the cellar getting soft and here you make an applecake with just one apple. But bad, it's not." Opoe took another bite.

A great deal of snow fell that month. It was so still outside that I could hear almost everything that went on. People walking by, their wooden shoes making crunchy noises. The little Groothuis boy. When his father came home from work, he pulled him on a sled. "Dad, run faster; you can do it." A few seconds later the little boy laughed and laughed. He must have fallen backward in the snow.

I could pull him, and he wouldn't have to wait till his father came home. All I'd have to do was to cross the street. Why couldn't I? Slowly I got up. Crazy. Everything.

"D'you girls know that tomorrow you've been here a year? Eh?"

"Yes, Johan, we know." How could we not know?

"How d'you like it here after a year?"

"Fine." Stop it, Johan.

"That's a girl!"

"Johan, do we stay up till midnight?"

"No, I can't see staying up New Year's Eve with no glass of beer. Boy, if the war's over next year I'm going to drink enough for a couple of New Year's Eves. How about you, wife?"

"Ah, Johan, I don't drink. You know that."

"Ja, ja," Johan said, "I know you're no fun. Hey,

Sini, you've hardly said a word all evening, what're you thinking about?"

"Nothing," Sini answered, without looking up.

"Well, Happy New Year everybody," Johan said. "Maybe 1944 will be better."

Ja, ja, Happy New Year.

Again.

9

Johan walked into our room. "Hey, girls, somebody's here to see you."

To see us? Who?

"Come in," he said, turning to a man behind him. "This, girls, is the man who has Rachel in his house. Yep, Reverend Slomp."

Speechlessly we stared at him. What was he doing here?

Rachel wanted to come for a few days, he said. She couldn't stand it any longer. She had to see us.

Dientje started to cry. "Johan, don't let her. It's too dangerous."

"Don't worry," he answered. "I know."

The Reverend Slomp said that Dientje was right, but Rachel wanted to come anyway.

"Can she?" Sini asked. "Please?"

I sat down on Johan's lap. "I want to see her," I coaxed.

Dientje warned Johan again. "What'll people say, Johan, if they see her walk in here. It's not the same as with Miss Kleinhoonte and the minister here. Rachel's Jewish!"

"She'll come at night," the Reverend Slomp said, "when it's dark."

"Johan, it's not right. What if there's another search, then what? If the Germans catch us, Johan, that's it."

"If the girls want to see her so badly, Johan," Opoe said.

I put my arms around his neck. Roughly Johan pushed me off his lap. "It's the goddamnedest thing to have to say yes to," he complained.

I looked at Sini. Guiltily we turned our heads away.

I remembered how neat Rachel was. Just plain dusting wouldn't be good enough for her. I rubbed the chairs instead. Out of my way, Sini, I'm busy. Beautiful. Rachel would like it.

The night she was going to come, the wind was howling. It was real March weather. We all sat upstairs waiting for her. Johan was the first one to hear her knock against the window. Rachel! We ran downstairs. "How are you?" I didn't pull away when she kissed me again and again.

"Dientje, put on some water for tea," Opoe said.

Dientje looked dazed. Without waiting for her, Opoe filled the kettle.

"How long did it take you to get here?" Johan asked.

"About five hours."

"Did you have any trouble?"

Well, she said, not trouble, but she did stop at someone's house to ask where the Oostervelds lived. She explained where it had been.

"Goddammit," Johan said angrily, "you shouldn't have done that. He's such a talker. Did he ask you anything?"

Anxiously we looked at Rachel. She shook her head. No.

"Well," Johan said, "you'll have to squeeze in the hiding place, too, in case there's going to be trouble."

Dientje sloshed tea over the table as she poured Rachel a cup. "How long are you staying?"

She was leaving tomorrow night after dark, Rachel answered in a subdued voice.

We went upstairs. Rachel hugged me. "It's so nice to be with my little sister again."

I'd better tell her tomorrow not to think of me as a little sister anymore. It could wait till tomorrow though.

When I peered over the edge of the bed, I could almost see two heads on the mattress, Sini and Rachel's. Nice.

What was the matter with Rachel? She answered every question in only a couple of words. "Do you mind being by yourself?"

"I don't."

Didn't she have more to say than that? Was she

angry? She didn't seem to be, but why then? Was it because she was always by herself with nobody to talk to? But Sini and I didn't always talk. Sometimes I had to start a fight with Sini, just to get her to speak to me. Then she'd say plenty. It was better than nothing, better than being alone.

I walked over to Rachel and sat on her lap. Almost twelve wasn't that old.

Had we heard from Father lately? she asked. Yes. He was hungry all the time. The only thing he ever wrote about was food, what he used to eat and what he was planning to eat after the war.

Rachel laughed. That's what he wrote to her, too, she said. It was nice to see her laugh again.

"Here's water, girls." Dientje put the bowl on the table. "I put in a little more. I figured there's three of you. You need anything, Rachel?"

"No, thank you."

"Okay then."

"Sini, is that all the water you ever get?" Rachel asked after Dientje left.

"On Saturday we get a pail instead of a bowl."

"For the weekend, I take it. Well, well. Annie, do you want me to wash your face?"

"No," I said indignantly. "What's the matter with you?"

She looked hurt. I felt bad about it, but my goodness!

We stood around the bowl, passing the towel to each other. I was pale, Rachel complained. Maybe I should take codliver oil. And why did we look so sloppy? Look at what we were wearing! Wasn't there an iron in the house?

How come Rachel had so much to say all of a sudden? Sullenly I walked away from her.

"Annie, come back. Now turn around again."

She hadn't been wrong, she said. Just what she thought, I didn't walk right. Well, I knew that. What else?

Didn't Sini make me exercise?

Yes, yes, she did, dammit. Had she only come to criticize us? What was that?

"Rachel, please take her with you. I'm tired of fighting with her."

Well, so was I. Maybe I *would* leave Sini, and go with Rachel. Oh, she couldn't take me? Fine. I wouldn't have gone anyway. I just thought it, to . . . to think something. I hated both of them.

"You girls having a nice time? That's good, that's good. Rachel, you eat an egg?"

"Sure, Opoe."

"Laid early this morning. I went in specially to see if they'd been busy, and yes, one of 'em had. Girls, you'll have one on Sunday. You didn't make such a trip. Fui-fui. Well, it's nice for them. You being here. You must have a lot to say to each other."

I was trying as hard as I could to say something to Rachel. Maybe I should show her where we lived in the summer.

"Follow me," I said mysteriously. I opened the door

of the back room wide. "Here. You see those windows? The left one's mine. And see that tree over there? It already has buds. That's very early." I looked up at her. What did she think of that?

She liked the room, she said, but wouldn't I let her iron my dress. I'd look so much better. "C'mon, Annie, it'll just take a minute."

"No," I said miserably.

When we got back to the other room, Rachel opened her bag and took out a postcard. Sini and I bent over it. The card was from Uncle Phil. "We're all on our way to Poland, but we'll manage. I'm going to throw this postcard out of the window at the next station in the hope that somebody will pick it up and mail it." Here the handwriting changed. It was now shaky. "Our warm clothes are coming in handy," Grandmother wrote, "because the weather is getting colder. Don't worry about us."

Don't worry about us. Sure. I knew what must've happened to them after they got off the train. I looked at Rachel out of the corner of my eye. She knew, too, or she wouldn't have looked so solemn.

When it was dark outside, Rachel got ready to leave. Silently she hugged us. Her face was wet. So was mine. Why did she have to go so soon? We hadn't even started to talk to each other, not really.

She left our room and closed the door behind her. Quickly she ran down the stairs. After a moment Sini went into the back room. I heard her crying through the doors.

We should have asked Rachel where in Winterswijk we'd meet after the war. We couldn't very well meet by our house. NSB-ers were living in it. Wouldn't they have to leave when we got back though? Of course. Run, we'd say. Sure. They couldn't do anything to us then.

But when would after the war be? The Germans had been losing for years now. All right, for a year and a half. How long could they go on losing without giving up? I walked up and down the room. I might just as well. When would this war be over, eh? When?

So at night Allied planes destroyed German cities. Very impressive. The Russians were fighting near the Polish border. Big deal, Poland. Only Johan thought it was a big deal. "All the Russians have got to do now is cross Poland and go right into Germany. Boy!" Boy! was right. And the Americans and the British were still fighting in Italy as if they were never going to stop. They probably liked it there. Nice climate or something. Why would they bother to come this way? Just look out the window. All that rain. I kicked the table leg as I passed it. Damned table leg.

Sini hadn't even heard. She was talking to Johan. "I can't imagine that you have any of our money left," she said. "Father never thought we'd have to stay this long."

"I don't."

"What now, Johan?"

"What d'you mean, what now? Nothing, of course. You think I'm turning you out in the street 'cause you've got no more money, eh?"

"Father'll pay you after the war, Johan."

"Well, I don't know about that. In the first place he's got to live through it, and in the second place he may not have any more money. But don't worry. He can always buy me a cow or two real cheap. Or sell a few of mine for more than they're worth. Eh, Johan isn't such a fool. For a dumb farmer."

"Oh, Johan!"

"Sini, they're saying the invasion's coming soon."

"Who's they, Johan?"

"At the bleachworks. That man I work with is sure the war won't go on much longer. And I'll tell you why he thinks so."

"Stop it, Johan," Sini said wearily, "I don't care what he thinks of the situation."

Why didn't Sini let Johan tell us why the man thought there'd be an invasion soon? Maybe he knew something we didn't know. That could be. Ah, no, she was probably right. I sighed.

With difficulty I got up and went to the back room. I stopped when I reached the window. Indifferently I noticed that the trees were green again. Soon we'd be back in this room, for the summer. No, not again. Please!

High heels were clicking on the street outside. I pushed my chair away from the window. I knew it was nine o'clock without looking at the watch. Every morning at this time, Mrs. Groothuis came to get milk, just like last summer. She knocked at the kitchen door. "*Hoo-oo,* anybody home?"

She never stayed long. And when she walked home, she went much slower, so she wouldn't spill any milk.

If the mailman came it would be shortly afterward. I had to listen carefully for him. He came on the bike, and I couldn't tell he was there until he jumped off it right under my window. I winked at it. You know something, stupid window, we may not have to be here that much longer. Nope. Not after last night's news: ALLIED TROOPS LANDED IN NORMANDY.

I mouthed the word *Normandy* again. You probably don't know where that is, right? Just like Opoe. "That in Italy again?" she had asked. That Opoe. Nope, it's in France, and this is the invasion the man in Boekelo and Johan and everybody were talking about. You didn't know that either, did you? I grimaced at the window. And you know something else? Johan and Sini bet that we'll be free by August. Yes, this August. So, let's see, it's June now, in two months I may not be sitting here all day keeping you company. You'll be on your own again. "Right Sini?"

Sini looked puzzled. How could she respond? I hadn't been talking to her. She was probably thinking about getting a tan. What had Opoe said about that last night? "We get a tan whether we want it or not. Bah, nonsense!"

"In Normandy the weather's supposed to be awful today," Johan said. "Nothing but rain."

"Poor things, having to fight in that weather. Fui-fui."

"Let's go to bed," Dientje said. "I've got a headache already from all that news."

"Awright, wife. But if this gives you a headache, boy, what'll you have when the Allies get to Usselo, eh? Those Americans and English and Canadians?"

"They'd come here? To Usselo?"

"Of course, they will. You better start learning, eh— What do they talk in America and England, Sini? And in Canada?"

"English."

"Yep, English. Goddammit, Sini, I want you to teach me some."

"English. What's next. Johan, don't act so silly," Opoe said. "For a grown man. . . ."

"Stay out of it, Ma. How d'you say, *Hebben jullie sigaretten?*"

"Do you have cigarettes?"

Johan tried it. His tongue stumbled over the words. Dientje laughed. "Stop it, Johan. You sound like a dumb farmer."

Johan didn't answer. He tried it again and sounded much better this time. And again. That was it. He now pronounced the words just like Sini.

"I want to be sure I can say it right. I'm sick of my own tobacco."

"Annie," Sini said worriedly, "I've been watching you for quite a while, and I don't like what I see. You're mumbling and carrying on as if you have an audience."

I smiled at her. But I did have an audience. I turned my head back to the window and winked. All right, Sini, I know what you want me to do. Exercise. Energetically I got off the chair. C'mon legs, a little higher. Ow. So they hurt, but it's good for you. You don't want anyone to point at you after the war. Ha, that sounded good—after the war. I'd better practice my English, too. After all, wouldn't *I* want to talk to the soldiers, too? Of course.

Opoe asked a good question the other day. "How far have those soldiers gotten?" Very good question. Not very far. But they're doing all right. Of course, of course. They like France. Apparently.

I spent long hours looking at the window. It was better than looking at Sini's face. The last time she laughed was when the radio started to say that somebody had tried to kill Hitler. And even then she only laughed for a few seconds—until she heard that all he got was a couple of scratches. Anyway, that was weeks ago, before August, before Johan and Sini lost their bet. Even the fact that most of France was liberated couldn't take Sini's mind off a tan. "Again I won't get one this summer, Annie. Look at me, as pale as ever."

Maybe we could ask Johan whether he'd let us go out for an afternoon. "Sini?"

"You're crazy."

Well, we could ask. Where could we go though?

"A few more fine days like this one," Dientje said, "and we can cut the wheat. It came up nicely this year, thick and tall."

"Where's the wheat field?"

"In back of the shed." Dientje looked out the window. "No, you can't see it from here. But it's there all right."

Sini and I looked at each other. When would Johan be home?

"It looks so beautiful outside, Johan. Please?"

"I want to tell you girls something. You got me to say yes when you wanted Rachel here, but this time I'm not going to be such a sucker."

"Girls," Dientje said, pulling me on her lap. "What if somebody saw you. We could all end up dead. Think of that. Please don't ask'm again." She put her arms around my waist. I loosened them.

"Just for a tan," Opoe said. "No, that I can't see."

"But Johan, it would be so nice to be out during the day again. It's been. . . ."

"That's enough, girls."

"Two years, Johan. And that's a long time."

The next day Johan asked us if we were ready. We stared at him. What for?

"Didn't you ask me last night about going out? Eh?"

Well, we had, but he had said no.

"So I changed my mind. Sini, I'll take you downstairs first. Annie, you wait here. I'll be back for you."

I felt the blood rise to my cheeks. Did he mean it? He must have. He and Sini were already heading for the door.

I tapped my foot on the floor. We were going out in broad daylight. Well, you'd have to if you wanted to

141

get a tan. Right, window? And what a beautiful day it was, not one cloud.

I hopped over to the window. There was Johan, pushing a wheelbarrow. But he was by himself. Sini would probably come out of the kitchen in a minute. Would she just walk over to the wheat field though? What was that in the wheelbarrow? I pushed my nose against the window. All I could see was a horse blanket. Did it cover something? Sini perhaps?

I strained my eyes. That bulge could be her.

A few minutes later Johan came back with the wheelbarrow. The blanket lay flat and wrinkled in the bottom.

"Annie, you can come down."

The wheelbarrow was standing in the kitchen.

"Get in. I'll cover you up."

"If you knew how dangerous this is," Dientje said in a fearful voice.

"Fui-fui. Hendrik should see that people have to go out in wheelbarrows and covered up."

Slowly I pulled up my legs until they almost touched my face. I put both hands over my right cheek to keep the rough blanket off my face. Somebody opened the door. The iron band around the wheel made scraping sounds on the walk.

"*Ksshht*. Out of the way you," Johan hollered. The chickens, of course. I smiled. Good for them to have to get out of the way for me.

It was warm. I raised my arm a little to let some air in. "Annie," Johan hissed. Immediately I put it down again. Dumb of me.

Johan stopped, then with great force he pushed the wheelbarrow into the wheat field. He stopped again. This time he took the blanket off.

There was Sini sitting on a bed of flattened wheat stalks. With difficulty I climbed out of the wheelbarrow. The wheat was taller than I was. Johan spread the blanket on the ground. "Well, here you are, girls. And you've got all day. I'll be back for you around suppertime."

We lay down on our backs, to get our faces tanned. I put my arms under my head. Contentedly I felt a little bit of wind on my face. Isn't it nice to be here, as if we're free? The wheelbarrow? What about it? That wasn't such a bad ride, a little bumpy maybe. I know this is not a real beach, but there aren't all those people either, kicking sand in your face. And no boys to take Sini away from me. What was she saying? That she was going to leave Winterswijk after the war?

"Why, Sini?"

It was a boring town, she said. It had dances on Saturday nights only. I'd better enjoy today, having her all to myself. I tried to open my eyes, but the sun hurt. Cautiously I opened one eye, then the other one. I put my hands over them to keep all that light out. Then I spread my fingers apart so that I could see something. The sky was so blue. And not one cloud. Wasn't it nice to be out? "Sini?"

"Ahem," she said in a lazy voice.

I turned on my side to look at her. Her face was all sweaty. It didn't matter, she said, that's how all tans started.

A plane flew over. It sounded as if it were skimming the tops of the wheat stalks. What would the pilot think if he could see us? We pulled the blanket over us and stayed perfectly still, until we could no longer hear the plane.

When was Johan coming back again? At suppertime? "Why that late, Sini?"

"Are you bored already?"

"No, of course not."

It was getting awfully warm though. A pity there wasn't any shade. I wiped my arms across my face. Wet. Now before the war Mother would've called me inside after this many hours in the sun. I would've complained. "You never let me do anything." But I would've gone in, relieved.

It would be nice to be back upstairs now, to sit in front of the window and look at the trees, to walk to the other room if I felt like walking. I had had enough of this. *E-n-o-u-g-h,* enough. I stuck my lower lip out and blew against my nose. Hot day.

All of a sudden Sini pushed me deeper into the wheat. What was the matter? She pointed to the right where the wheat stalks were swaying wildly. Somebody was coming.

"Girls, where are you?"

Johan. Of course, it was after five.

"My god, you got too much sun. Poor things." He looked upset. "And listen to this. Dientje's sister and the child are here. I can't take you back until they've left. And I don't know when that'll be." He sat down next to us. "Goddammit, what did I do? You feel all right? I'm going back to the house. We'll see if they can't leave soon."

A half hour later he came back, this time with the wheelbarrow. "Annie, get in."

"Johan, don't put that blanket on me. It hurts too much."

"I know, but it's got to be done. Let's go."

I put my hands over my face again. Johan almost ran. With every step the blanket chafed my arms and legs. The kitchen door opened. I was back.

"God-o-god-o-god, Johan, what did you do to them?"

"I told you not to take'm out, Johan, but you never listen to me. You always listen to them." Dientje bent over me. "And he thinks he's so smart."

"Dientje, leave Johan alone," Opoe said. "Hollering at him doesn't help the girls. Get some wet towels."

"I'm cold, Sini."

"Cold?" Sini asked in a nervous voice. "You can't be. Let me feel your face. You're not cold, you're burning hot."

But I was shivering.

"Johan, she needs a doctor," Sini said.

"We really don't know one. Last time we had the one in Boekelo was at least ten years ago when Ma had pneumonia."

"More, Johan, I wasn't sixty yet. And I didn't like 'm. He was a blabbermouth."

"Ma, you don't like any doctors."

"He was no good," Opoe said firmly. "We can't go to 'm."

"Who are we going to get then?" Johan asked.

"Go to the Hanninks," Dientje suggested. "Maybe they'll know one who won't talk."

Johan and Opoe looked at her in surprise. I turned over on the bed. Ouch.

When the doctor came he said it was a miracle that Sini wasn't sick, too, after that many hours in the sun. He sounded angry.

"He was a nice enough man," Opoe said after he left, "for a doctor."

"You mad at me, Annie?" Johan asked. "I couldn't get you earlier, or I would've."

"I'm not mad, Johan."

"Good night, Annie," Opoe said. "If you need anything, just call me. I'm awake anyway."

"She can call me," Dientje said. "I'm closer to her."

"Move over, Dientje, so she has more space," Johan said.

"Good night, little sister." Carefully Sini kissed me.

It really had been a nice day. A little long though. And hot.

10

THE Allies were running through Belgium, just like that. They would be in Holland next, the radio said. Every time I thought about it, I had to smile. If it was wonderful to be almost free, how wonderful it would be when the Allies really came. Wasn't Holland only a little bigger than Belgium? Say a few days' worth? Many people living in the south of Holland, near the Belgian border, could probably see the Allied soldiers already. They were lucky.

I turned to Opoe. "Will you come and see us when we're back in Winterswijk?" I asked her.

"Me?" She laughed. "No. I haven't been any place in twenty-one years. Winterswijk. What's next?"

"I'll come," Johan said, "and I won't be wearing these dumb overalls. I'll wear my suit."

"Johan, you're late for work again," Opoe said.

"Yes, Johan, hurry," Dientje urged.

"Dammit, I've got too many women in the house."

He slammed the door when he left.

While Johan was on his way to Boekelo, Mr. Hannink came to see us. A truck was going from house to house, he said, checking.

"Checking what?" Dientje gasped, but Mr. Hannink had already gone.

Sini and I got into the hiding place as fast as we could.

"God-o-god-o-god, Dientje, don't close it yet."

"But they'll be here any minute. Mr. Hannink said so."

"You stay up here and sit in front of the window. When you see that truck, you close the opening to the hiding place."

"Where are *you* going?"

"To the kitchen, of course. Where else? Johan's coming home at twelve to eat."

Sini and I stood close together, listening, waiting for Dientje to come.

"Okay, okay." Dientje ran over to us. "They're here. They're here."

She closed up the hiding place with the piece of wood. We heard her lower the shelf and close the closet door. We heard her footsteps as she ran down the stairs. Then nothing.

Where were they? What took them so long? We could suffocate in here if they didn't come for a long time. I leaned up against Sini.

Footsteps. Loud ones. Boots. Coming up the stairs. Wooden shoes. Coming behind. Sini put her arms around me and pushed my head against her shoulder.

Loud voices. Ugly ones. Furniture being moved. And Opoe's protesting voice. The closet door was thrown open. Hands fumbled on the shelves. Sini was trembling. She tightened her arms around me. I no longer breathed through my nose. Breathing through my mouth made less noise.

A man was speaking German. Then another was saying, "We want to know where all those pieces of material come from."

"What's he doing? He can't just take all of that. It's mine," Opoe said. "Tell'm that."

A stick pounded once on the floor, and then again. The closet door was slammed. My heart was beating too loudly. What if they could hear us? Would they stick a bayonet through the closet wall? They could. All over the wall, to be sure to hit whoever was behind the wall.

My mouth was dry, yet I didn't dare breathe through my nose. They might still be there. But you clearly heard them storm down the stairs, didn't you? I know, but what if they had left a soldier behind? Sini must think so, too, or she wouldn't be holding me so tightly.

There were noises on the stairs again. They're coming back? No, only wooden shoes this time.

"They're gone, girls." Dientje removed the piece of wood. "We were lucky. One of 'em was standing right here. I was afraid he would hear you breathe."

We didn't move. Dientje bent in front of the hole. "They're gone."

"Girls, I brought you a drop of coffee," Opoe said. "You can come out now. They were nasty people. They took the pig we were going to kill, and the cloth I've been saving for years."

Pig? Cloth? It could have been us.

"No, Opoe, we'll stay in here this morning. They might come back."

"If you hadn't nagged me out of the house, I'd have been here. Now you see," Johan said when he heard about the search. "You let them take that pig away? Fools, you are. Ma, you should've stopped them."

"Johan, don't yell at me. I did want to stop them, but Dientje here was awfully scared."

"I was not."

"Dientje, I saw you. . . ."

"Well," Johan said, "I've got to go back to the bleachworks."

"No, Johan, stay home this afternoon."

"What d'you mean? I've got to go to work. I've been late too many times."

"But, Johan, what if they come back?"

"That's why you want me to stay? Eh? To—what d'you call it—protect you?"

"Yes."

"Okay, I will. I almost wish they'd come back. I'd tell them a thing or two. I'd get the pig back too, I bet. Okay, okay, I won't talk about it anymore. At least they didn't find the girls."

Sometime in the afternoon, Dientje ran in. "Remember when I took you to the farmer with the ten Jews? Mimi was one of them? Remember, Annie, you didn't talk to her?" Her voice trembled. "The Germans found 'em. They took everybody in the house away on the truck. The farmer and his wife, too. Everybody."

"Weren't the Jews in the hiding place?"

"Yes, but that's where they were found. You see now how careful you've got to be? Because if they get you, that's it."

"Yes, Dientje."

I licked my lips. They felt cracked.

I remembered Mimi. She hadn't talked to me either.

Mimi no longer had to stay inside . . . she was probably even traveling . . . sure she was . . . on that train.

My lips *were* cracked.

It was very late and very dark when Mr. Hannink came again to the house. He had something important to ask Johan, he said, something that had to do with the farmer and the ten Jews who had been caught.

"Sit down," Johan said solemnly.

"Somebody tipped off the Germans," Mr. Hannink said. "They knew all those Jews were there and where their hiding place was." He spoke in an even lower voice. "And I know who that somebody was."

We were looking at his mouth. What was he going to say next?

He cleared his throat. "That man has to be killed before he does more harm." His eyes rested on Johan. "Could you do it?"

Dientje walked over to Johan. Menacingly she stood in front of him.

"Well," Johan said hesitantly, "to tell you the truth, Mr. Hannink, I've actually never killed anyone before."

"God-o-god-o-god," Opoe said.

It wouldn't be difficult, Mr. Hannink explained. "I'll give you a revolver. You can hide yourself in the ditch next to his house and wait for him to come out. As soon as you've shot him, you get away."

Slowly Johan shook his head. "If anything happened to me, the women here would go crazy," he said.

Dientje went back to her chair.

A few days later a boy came over. He wanted to talk to Oosterveld about a job that had to be done, he said. He showed Johan a note signed by Mr. Hannink.

He stayed for a little while, then left with the revolver and the instructions that Mr. Hannink had given to Johan.

It only took a day. The Germans were furious. Why had such a good man been shot? To show how furious they were, they arrested several people. We'll let them go, they said, as soon as the killer of our friend has turned himself in.

When he didn't, the hostages were found along

Usselo's main road, shot. Their fingers had been broken.

It made us very quiet, especially Johan.

In the middle of September thousands of British parachutists were dropped at Arnhem.

"You know, you can get from Arnhem to Usselo on the bike in one day?" Johan said. "Yep, if you have big legs like Dientje."

Sini laughed. While she was helping Johan with his English, I looked at her. Her face was flushed. I felt like crying. Remember how long they fought in Italy, Sini? Months. Why do you always forget these things? I know Arnhem is in Holland. Still. . . . Tomorrow you may be miserable again.

In less than ten days it was all over. No, not the war, just the fighting. More German soldiers were in Arnhem than the Allies had thought, and the Allied soldiers that came up through the south of Holland to help the paratroopers had to go back. But not all the way back. Part of the south of Holland remained free, the part of Holland Usselo was not in. People in Eindhoven were probably singing and dancing and shouting.

The Allies should have freed the rest of Holland, too. We all wanted to get rid of the Germans. The soldiers were becoming nastier and nastier, and people were more scared than ever—almost everybody—about everything.

One night soldiers had marched into movie houses

in Amsterdam. They had turned on the lights so that they could see which men were young enough to go to Germany. So much work still had to be done for Germany, and there were not enough Germans to do it. Not enough Jews, either. But there were still Dutch Gentile men around. After that night men stopped going to the movies, but it didn't matter. The soldiers looked in other places: in churches, on trains. If they were angry at not finding enough men to take away, they shot people in the streets. They had done it. When Johan tried to tell Sini what the man he worked with thought the Allies would do next, she started to scream. When I walked over to her, she turned her back on me.

And the rain continued, as if it were never going to stop. Leaves were fluttering around aimlessly and landing on the ground in soft, slippery piles. A few stuck against the window and stayed there, forming a pattern.

It was getting chilly, and there was no longer any coal. At night we went down to the kitchen to get warm. "Johan, are you sure nobody can see through the shades?" Dientje asked every time.

But who'd be there to look? Nobody was allowed out after dark anymore. "So, who'd come, eh?"

It was cozy in the kitchen. The oven door was open. Sini's and my feet were resting on it. Opoe got up and stuck her hand into the oven for a piece of dry wood. With a bent wire she tried to remove a disk from the top of the stove. "Fui-fui, with just that oil lamp I can't really see what I'm doing. No electricity at night. What's next? Industry needs it. Pooh, industry. What's the matter with houses?"

"Ma, I remember what you used to say. 'Electricity, pooh. That's for young people. For the few years I'm going to be around, oil lamps suit me fine.' How many years ago did you say that?"

"Ja, ja. I can't help it."

"Johan," Dientje said, "I don't know what to do with all those city people who come to the door for food. Six today. They said they were lucky they could still drag themselves around. People are lying in the streets, starved to death, they said."

"God-o-god-o-god, Johan, they're so thin."

"What did you give them?"

"A couple of potatoes each," Dientje said. "You know they wanted to give me a lot of money for them?"

"Don't take it."

"I didn't."

"It's a disgrace. So many farmers charge all they can get away with. It's a scandal."

"Now's when you get to know people. And, boy, most of 'em are no good." Opoe shook her head.

"But I didn't, Johan," Dientje said.

"A goddamned scandal."

"A few came from that town where they were fighting, Johan. Arnhem. That whole town's a ruin, they said. People from there are just wandering around Holland. Fui-fui, and with winter coming."

Johan scratched his head. "Damn, it's that we've got

the girls, or I'd say let some of them sleep in the garage. But we can't have any strangers poking around."

Out in the street a car stopped suddenly. The gate opened and loud footsteps sounded at the side of the house. Boots. Johan pushed us upstairs. "Into the hiding place, fast."

My goodness, what a long time. Weren't they coming? What was going on?

"Sini," I whispered.

"Hush."

Hush for what? I shifted my weight from one leg to the other. The closet was getting stuffy.

The Germans had not come back to search the house again, Johan told us after they had left. They had come to tell him that they needed part of the house for their headquarters. "Look, I said, you don't want to live here. We haven't got running water. We haven't even got a decent toilet. But it didn't matter. Well, I said, upstairs is out, you wouldn't want to climb those steep stairs. The only thing that makes sense is to let you have the three rooms in front of the house. I showed them the rooms, and they said they were fine." Noisily Johan blew his nose. "Damn. And I bet they'll be here day and night."

My hands felt clammy. I stared at my feet. They were ugly, not the kind of feet I read about in books.

"Well," Sini said, "what now? Do you think Mr. Hannink can find us another place?"

"Eh? What d'you mean? You're going to stay here. What else? Right, Dientje?"

"You'll have to be very careful," Dientje said, "but we wouldn't send you away."

"I'll tell you something: you're going to be pretty safe here. As long as you don't make any noise. Because what fool would search our house for Jews? Eh? Nobody. Ha, ha, Germans and you in the same house! How's that for a dumb farmer?" Johan wiped the tears from his eyes.

"But Johan," Dientje said, "what if they come up the stairs?"

"I thought of that. I'm closing those three rooms off from the rest of the house, so nobody can get through that way. The only other way they can get to the stairs is through the kitchen. Either you or Ma have got to be there all day."

"But what if they go up anyway?"

"Dientje," Opoe warned, "keep your wits together."

"How long are they going to be here?" Sini asked.

"How could I have asked them that? Till the end of the war maybe."

That could be a long time. Nothing new was happening.

"You'll have to stay in the back room all day because the front room's right over their offices."

"But, Johan, they'll freeze in there. That's the coldest room in the house."

"They'll have to stay in bed then."

"The radio, Johan," Sini said.

"Goddammit. We can't hear the news anymore. I'll have to take the radio out of that place and put it somewhere else. Can't leave my radio in their office, can I?"

"Then how will we find out what's really going on, Johan?"

"Don't worry. I'll find out. What a hell of a thing to have—German headquarters. Ma, how's that for excitement?"

Opoe shook her head. "I don't like it. And then those telephones they'll put in. Telephones. What's next! Have you ever talked on one?" she asked Sini.

"Sure, Opoe."

"What's it like?"

"That's hard to explain."

"Ja, ja, I guess. If Hendrik knew."

"Johan, he said they were going to use the garage. Now, what if the girls come too close to the window? Johan, I want their hair dyed. That black hair is no good."

"How are we going to do that, woman?"

"Go to Mr. Hannink. Maybe he has some stuff for it."

He did. I hated myself with red hair. I was never going to go outside again. Not even when the war was over. Furiously I pushed my chair against the wall. I liked it here.

The next week the Germans moved in. At the same time Sini and I started to live in bed. October 17, 1944

—that's what the calendar said. The days were long, and silent. Evenings were just as long and silent. Sini hardly talked. Maybe she would if I made her mad enough, but how could we fight if we could only whisper?

Opoe brought our meals up in a towel. "In case I meet one of 'em. They keep coming in the kitchen. For coffee, all kinds of things. Oh, my God, what's that noise?"

"That's the telephone."

"You can hear it all the way up here? Boy, that's scary stuff. I better go downstairs."

Where it was warm. To them. What kind of head-quarters was this anyway? Where they went in and out of the kitchen all the time, day and night, drinking coffee. I stuffed my pillow in my mouth and bit it until I felt nauseous.

Would they never go away? Restlessly I rolled around the bed.

"Watch it, I have a needle in my hand."

Didn't Dientje have the time to mend socks? After all, she sat in that kitchen all day. "Sini, don't you think so, too?"

"Yes," she said. "How dare they have fun with those soldiers. One of them even calls Opoe 'Opoe.' He gave her chocolates. Sure, we ate them, but she shouldn't take anything from them. And Johan is boasting that he's learning so much German. I'm out of wool." Her voice had become more and more annoyed. "And I wanted to finish this sock. Now I'll have to wait till

Dientje comes up here with more wool sometime today."

She threw the sock down. "We're always waiting for somebody." She sobbed in her pillow. "I can't stand it any longer, Annie."

Well, why should she? I sat up.

"Where are you going?"

"Downstairs to get some wool."

She grabbed my arm. "Let go, Sini." How was I going to do it? "Leave it to me," I said, imitating Johan. "Sure, I'll be careful. I'm not crazy."

Carefully I got out of bed and crawled to the door. With difficulty I stood up. I moved my legs up and down a little bit. They ached. Four weeks in bed was a long time.

"Did you change your mind?"

"No, I just have to wait a few minutes before I can walk."

"Come back to bed and forget it. I can wait."

"No, no, I'm fine."

There, I was through the door. It was chilly. I shivered in my pajamas. It would actually be nice to go back to bed. Later I would, after I got the yarn. I grabbed the railing. Hesitantly I lowered one foot, then the other one. I put my weight on them only when they were both together on the same step. Next. Very well. Halfway down. I stopped a minute. The only sound came from their typewriter. Good, they were in the front. Well, maybe I could go a little faster then. My legs felt better, too. Walking could only be good for me.

There. I was at the bottom of the stairs. I put my hand on the doorknob and looked through the glass part of the door. Was anybody on the other side of it? No, no one. I probably picked a very good time to do this job. As quickly as I could, I crossed the room. Well, that wasn't so bad, was it? I put my cheek against the kitchen door. Nobody seemed to be there.

Wait a minute. That was Johan's voice. "What d'you think, Ma, are we going to get snow today?"

"We could. My head hurts an awful lot."

Then nothing. Dientje must not be in the kitchen. Maybe I should go back upstairs and try again later? No, Opoe probably knew where the wool was.

"We've got very little hay this winter. We're going to have a tough time."

"Ja, ja, I guess so."

Obviously there wasn't anybody in the kitchen but Opoe and Johan.

I touched the doorknob. I swallowed. Slowly I pushed the door open. And then faster. I stuck my head into the kitchen.

I only saw one face. It stuck out from a uniform. German.

I turned around, crossed the room, and went up the stairs.

"Didn't you get any yarn?" Sini asked. "Look at me, something's wrong with you. What happened? Did you get to the kitchen? Answer me."

I stood by the door.

"Tell me what happened. Were they angry?"

I didn't move.

"Annie, what's going on? Come here." Sini was no longer whispering.

I couldn't move.

"Did you see Dientje?"

I shook my head. No.

"Who *did* you see. One of *them*?"

I nodded.

"Where."

"In the kitchen."

"But why did you go in there if they weren't by themselves?"

I licked my lips. "I thought they were."

Sini got out of bed. "Let's get dressed. Hurry up."

"Why are we getting dressed?"

"They'll be up here any minute to take us away."

With trembling hands, she opened the drawer and took out some clothes. Without looking at each other, we put them on.

We sat down on the bed in street clothes and waited. I was not even afraid. I felt nothing.

Was that them? No, Johan walked in. "Boy, o boy, you scared me. It was a good thing Dientje was in the stable. What came over you?"

I studied my nails. They needed cutting.

"Eh? Answer me."

"Johan, when are they coming?" Sini asked.

"Who?"

"The soldiers."

"They're not coming."

I looked up.

"For a minute I thought, What the hell's going on? I couldn't believe my eyes. There she was in her pajamas. Who's that little girl, the German asked, and why is she so scared? And then I came out with something pretty clever. I said, Oh, that's Rikie, Dientje's niece. She's been here for a day or two, and she's awfully shy. Maybe she'll come out later before she goes home.

"So as soon as I could get away, I went to the stable to tell Dientje about it. Boy! So quit sniveling, I said to her. Go to your sister and get the little girl. You can be back in a little over an hour. But she's in school, she said. So what? I said to her. Go to the school and take her out.

"But my sister doesn't even know we've got Jews, she said. Well, I said, you've got to tell her. But Rikie doesn't look like Annie, Dientje said. She's right about that, but I figure the fellow didn't see you long enough to remember what you look like. What are you wearing those clothes for?"

"We thought they'd come upstairs and take us away."

"You didn't think I'd get you out of this mess? Eh? What's the matter with you?"

Funny to hear a girl's voice outside. What was her name again? Rikie? She should get together with the

Groothuis boy; then they could laugh together. Ha, ha, ha, little boy, what are you doing? Playing ball? That's not a good way. Let me show you how. No, go away. Ha, ha, ha.

I pulled my pajama sleeves down. Stupid kids. Bah. They don't know what is going on in the world. I'll bet they don't even know that Hitler is a maniac. I turned my back to the wall and stuck my fingers in my ears.

"I've got such a headache," Dientje said that night, "you can't imagine. What a day! And she didn't even know why she came with me."

"I had such a time keeping that little Rikie from going upstairs," Opoe said. "Fui-fui, she's a stubborn one. Nice enough though. It wasn't smart what you did, Annie. He could've been nasty and followed you. And then what?"

And then what? Why were the Germans in the kitchen all the time? That's what I wanted to know. Maybe they even ate there, off plates. Unhappily I stared into the dark room. It wasn't right.

A week later we were startled by a lot of noise coming from the office, as if the furniture was being pushed around. We listened tensely. They were probably making room for more desks, Sini said. "They must have spread the word about what a wonderful house this is."

Yes, and what a warm kitchen.

But we were wrong.

"They packed up their stuff," Johan panted, "and they left just like that. I'm glad. I was getting tired of having those fellows under foot all the time. Hey, Sini, I'm going to put the radio back in. Eh, for tonight?"

"Sure," she laughed. "Maybe the Allies are coming. Maybe that's why they left in such a hurry. I'll bet you that's what it is."

With wobbly steps I walked over to my window. It was covered with a layer of ice. I opened my mouth wide and breathed on it. Slowly the ice melted. I stopped when enough of the window was clear to let me see outside. Sky.

11

For a while the Germans had stopped pulling men out of public places. Instead the official daily newspaper that only came out three times a week now asked them to go to work for Germany. "We need you," it said. "You'll like the work, and we'll give you extra rations."

Some men were so hungry that they volunteered for the work, but not enough of them did, and trucks went around to pick them off the streets.

"Goddammit," Johan said, "I'm almost scared to go out. Next they'll come to the house. You know something? I'm going to hide, too."

"Fui-fui, Johan."

"With the girls upstairs?" Dientje asked.

"Na, woman, I couldn't sit up here all day, and I don't fit in the hiding place. Where would I go if they searched the house? No, I've got a plan that will be safe for everybody, especially for the girls." He blew thick spirals of smoke out of his nostrils.

In a small voice Dientje asked him where he was going to hide.

"In Enschede."

"O God-o-god-o-god, Johan, the city."

Mr. Hannink had a place for him there, Johan said, where the Germans wouldn't be likely to look. "It's in a firehouse. You know, Mr. Hannink would go there himself if he wasn't too old to have to worry about being picked up."

Dientje and Opoe looked at him unbelievingly.

"Really," Johan said, "I'll stay there with a couple of other guys and as soon as things calm down again I'll be back, of course. You know, it won't be much fun sitting in that place all day with those fire engines." He crushed his cigarette in an empty cup. "Damn."

"But what about the girls?" Dientje asked in a shrill voice.

"What about them?" Johan said. "Why should anything change just because I won't be here for a couple of days? Eh?"

Opoe nodded.

Dientje started to cry. "You've never been away, Johan."

"This is war, woman."

I looked around for my sweater. I was shivering.

That night Sini didn't sleep on the mattress on the floor. She got into bed with Dientje and me.

"I'm scared, girls," Dientje kept saying. "It's so dangerous, and with Johan gone. . . . Opoe's no help. Girls, you hear me?"

We tossed and turned. We had heard.

When Opoe came in to wake us up in the morning, we were already out of bed.

"Mother," Dientje said, "it's too dangerous having the girls now. It really is."

She should keep her wits together, Opoe said. What was different now? The chickens were still hungry. We had to eat. "And Johan? He'll be back."

All right, Dientje argued, but who knew when.

"Ja, that I don't know either."

Sini and I sat on our chairs, listening.

Dientje went on: ". . . dangerous . . . if . . . that's it . . . shot . . . those murder camps . . . ja, ja . . . what do *you* know. We'll take 'em back when Johan gets home again."

What was that? Where would we go? I bit hard on my lower lip.

"I'm going to ask the Hanninks to take 'em. They said two years ago we were only going to have them for a couple of weeks. They can stay in that hiding place they've got out back."

No, not there, Dientje. I can't go back there. Please. I looked up at Opoe. She wouldn't let her take us to the Hanninks. Opoe tried to stop her, but Dientje was firm. "I don't want to do it to them either, but it's only for as long as Johan's gone."

After a while Opoe relented, but she had tears in her eyes. "Fui-fui, what a world!"

Sini said nothing.

Dientje left.

With an embarrassed face she came back from the Hanninks'. "It's all right," she said, "you can go tonight. They'll bring food and everything you'll need to that place. Honestly, girls, I feel bad about it."

On her way out she tried to hug me, but I pulled away. I felt bad about it, too. Worse than bad. Why wasn't Johan here? He probably liked it in Enschede with all those fire engines.

After it got dark that night, we left. Dientje walked rapidly ahead of us. Now and then she slowed down so we could catch up with her.

We waited in the Hanninks' backyard while she rang their bell. A minute later she was back with Mr. Hannink. We followed him to where the ground felt a little elevated. There we stopped.

"It's better this way, girls," Dientje whispered. "Honestly."

Numbly Sini and I stepped forward and down.

Days looked just like nights, even with the flashlight.

At night Mrs. Hannink came with food for the next day. "If we had a hiding place in the house," she said every time, "believe me, we wouldn't let you stay here."

Sini cried a great deal. She was sure the Oostervelds would never take us back.

"But, Sini, Johan won't leave us here."

"Why not?" she said.

Yes, why not? "He won't, Sini. You'll see."

"See what?" she sobbed. "See nothing. Ever again.

When I get out of here, I've had it. I'm not going to stay hidden any longer, and I don't care what happens to me, either."

She wanted to go back to the Oostervelds', but she was not going to stay hidden? "Sini?" But she couldn't hear me. She was making too much noise. She'd better be careful. Crying sounds don't usually come from the ground. I leaned over to tell her. It helped—for a little while. What would happen to me if Sini didn't want to stay hidden? Worriedly I lay down.

Johan would probably be coming back soon, Mr. Hannink said. The Germans seemed to have stopped picking men off the streets for work.

On the tenth night he did. "I just got home," he said, "and, goddammit, you weren't there. I'm furious at those women. Are you crazy sitting here like a couple of moles? Come on out. We're going home."

Dazed we walked behind him. He had come.

Sini hadn't forgotten what she had said in the hiding place, that she was not going to stay inside anymore.

"But it won't be that much longer," Johan told her, "so quit talking that way."

But she didn't. Then in December the Allies were attacked in Belgium. They were too confused to fight back and for days they withdrew, chased by the Germans.

"That won't last," Johan said. "Everybody knows that."

What he said didn't make Sini stop crying though. Neither did Dientje's frantic "Hush, hush, be quiet for Godsake!"

"I've never heard such goings-on in my life. Fui-fui."

"But, Opoe, I'm twenty-three, and I want to go outside. I've had enough."

"What d'you want me to do about it. Eh? Tell me." Johan was breathing heavily.

We all stared at Sini. Yes, what did she want him to do?

Ask Mr. Hannink for false identification papers, she said at once. How did she dare? Hadn't that poor man risked his life enough for us? Well, maybe he wouldn't do it. Nobody said anything for a minute.

"There are so many people from Arnhem who have lost their homes. Johan, couldn't I be one of them? I don't look Jewish. Who would find out? You yourself have had people from there coming to the house, asking for food and a place to sleep."

I didn't dare look at Johan's face. I was too afraid to see what his reaction would be. "Dammit, Sini, you're really asking me something this time."

I looked up. Johan was shaking his head. "But it's not a bad idea. Actually, it's a very good one. I could get you a job as a maid near here. I can tell 'em how good you are with cows. I'll go to Mr. Hannink and see what he and I can do. Eh? How's that for a dumb farmer?"

"Won't it be dangerous?"

"Ah, woman, not the way I've planned it."

Opoe shook her head. "It's not very nice for Annie, Johan."

"Well, she's a different person. She can stand it, and Sini can't."

Is that so! Sure, I love living up here. Doesn't it show? My smile isn't wide enough? Here, is this one better? That's how much I love it. And every year my smile will get wider and wider because I'll love it more and more.

"What does Annie have to say?" Opoe asked.

"I think maybe it's a good idea," I said as loud as I could.

Sini got off her chair and put her arms around me.

Mr. Hannink said he could get the papers, and a few days later he brought them over. An underground worker in Enschede had printed them for him.

On the front Sini signed her new name, Sini te Broeke, right over her picture. On the inside, born March 2, 1922, in Arnhem; profession, maid.

Johan went to a few farmers and asked them the same thing, "You want a maid? This girl came to my house, but I haven't got work for her. Otherwise I'd keep her myself. She's got a pair of work hands on her, boy. And she's something with cows, I can tell you. She can milk 'em faster than you can sit down underneath them."

The third farmer said he could use somebody like that and Sini put her few clothes in a bag. "Annie, if you really don't want me to go, Johan can tell the farmer I won't come. Annie?"

It looked like snow. Maybe there'd be some for Christmas.

"It's all right with you? Honestly?" Her voice trembled.

I nodded. It might even snow tonight.

"Don't tell 'em about your milking diploma," Opoe warned. "They're not fancy."

"Okay," Johan said, "We'd better go. I'll walk you over."

"You want a piece of bread and a cup of milk before you go, Sini?"

"Ma, where d'you think she's off to?"

"I know, but she could still want something."

"Don't work too hard," Dientje said. "The more you do the more they want."

"She's got to do something or I'd be a liar. What d'you think they want her for, eh? For her red hair? So don't tell her to be like you are. Come, say good-bye to your sister."

I wanted to get up and give her a kiss, but I couldn't do it. Sini came to me.

She picked up her bag and walked to the door. She didn't turn around.

A minute later I heard her come out of the kitchen with Johan. I buried my head in my hands. It wasn't fair.

I spent most of the days in bed. I had promised Sini

I'd walk around every day, but I didn't. If she really cares that much, let her come back. She likes being on that farm. What did she say again last week? She misses me. Then why didn't she visit last night. I frowned.

"She forgetting you?" Opoe asked me.

"No," I said, "she's very busy."

"With what?" Opoe asked.

Work, of course. Tomorrow she'll be here, for Christmas dinner, and she'll stay all afternoon and all evening.

Those were Dientje's footsteps on the stairs. What did she want? "Move over," she said, "so I can sit here. What've you been doing with yourself?"

What a question! I tried to smile.

"Where d'you want Dientje to hang this new calendar."

"No place."

What for? To fill this one up, too, with marked-off days? Thanks. No.

At dinnertime the next day I walked slowly downstairs.

"Is the kitchen door locked?" Dientje asked.

"Yes."

"Now, Annie, the minute you hear anybody outside you run up the stairs. Here, sit near the door."

Sini sat down next to me. She took my hand. It felt hard. "Johan, d'you know the Wassinks? They're at the next farm."

"Of course, I know them. Why?"

"I went out with their son last night."

I looked down at my plate.

"Is that so," Opoe asked. "Already you're going out?"

"Well, my God," Sini said, "I haven't for years. I'm the right age for it, Opoe."

"Where did you go?" Dientje asked.

"Well, there's no place to go in Usselo. You know that. We just went for a walk. He's nice. He asked me over to his house on New Year's Eve."

"Maybe you should keep Annie company that night," Johan said.

"She doesn't have to," I protested.

"Well, I would come here, but you go to bed very early. Okay, I'll do both. I'll get here early in the evening. Did you know that Boekelo has a drama club?"

"What does that do?" Opoe asked.

"Oh, they get together on Saturday nights and rehearse a play or something. They want me to join."

"You going to?" Opoe asked suspiciously.

"I don't know yet."

"What d'you want to be in a play for? What's the matter with coming here on Saturday nights? Boys, plays. What's next?"

"Ma, she's old enough to know what she's doing."

"Ja, ja, maybe. Dientje, this rabbit's so tough my gums hurt. No, it doesn't matter. I don't need much, not at my age. I can suck it a little bit and get the taste. What else have you got?"

I looked at Sini. Her eyes were sparkling. No wonder boys were asking her out. She was beautiful.

"Hey, Annie, I hear something. Go upstairs. Take your plate. No, give it to me." Dientje ran into the kitchen with it.

I stood up. With my hand I pushed the chair away. Desperately I tried to get to the stairs. The footsteps sounded closer and closer to the window. I couldn't move. My legs hurt so.

"Go, what's the matter with you," Dientje cried.

Johan jumped up from his chair and grabbed me by the shoulders. Roughly he opened the door and pushed me up the stairs. Tears were rolling down my cheeks when I reached my room. What a terrible thing, not to be able to move. Everybody had stared at me, even Sini.

I threw myself on the bed. That's where I belonged. Not downstairs with the others. Hurriedly I sat up and wiped my face. Whoever was coming up the stairs didn't have to see me this way.

Sini came in. "You know, that was Groothuis. He came to tell Johan something he had just heard. The Allies have started a counterattack in Belgium. Isn't that great? Little sister, you may not have to sit here much longer. You know I think so much about you. Give me a kiss. I have to go."

"Will you come back tomorrow?" Why did I ask?

"I'll try. That's a promise."

I'll be more talkative tomorrow—if she comes. She will if she can. Her hands felt so rough. I know she works hard.

I heard the kitchen door close. I pressed myself against the wall next to the window and looked down from the corner of my eyes. It was Sini. She looked up. I smiled.

The Germans couldn't stop running. The Allies were chasing them right back into Germany. In the east, the Russians were doing the same thing; they had pushed the Germans back almost to Berlin.

When Sini came to see me, she pulled me out of bed. "Get up and move, Annie, and don't argue, not this time."

Would I be able to walk soon? Really walk? Outside? I started to smile. Anxiously I stuck my legs over the side of the bed. I was going to ask Dientje for that calendar for 1945. I had to cross off all the days in January and the first twenty-two in February. Every cold, endless one of them.

"You know that man I work with?"

"Yes, Johan, I know."

"He says the Canadian army's going to be here in a few weeks. Yep. Canadians. Show Johan how you can walk. Good girl."

Why is he talking about that man he works with again? Doesn't he even have a name? He has never been right yet. Never. He's . . . he's stupid . . . a liar. My lips started to tremble.

The man had been right about something. They were coming closer, the Canadians. But five weeks had gone by, and still they weren't here. And so little was happening upstairs. Outside, the trees were becoming green again, the pale gentle green of spring.

D'you see it, too, window? You must. You're as close to the trees as I am. Then tell me what it looks like to you. What, you're not answering? How dare you.

I went over to the window. Say something.

Disgustedly I walked away. What was the use?

On March 31 the Germans took every horse and cart they could lay their hands on.

"What would they do that for?" Opoe asked.

"So they can run faster," Johan answered.

"But if it doesn't belong to them?"

"Ma, haven't you learned anything in these five years?"

"Ja, ja, they're not honest, are they?"

Johan ran out of the house. He was going to take his horse to a safer place, where "they've got to be pretty clever to find her."

He'd better be careful, with all those airplanes going over. Could they be German? Were they attacking the Canadians? Pushing them back? I covered my ears. Where was everybody.

"Annie," Dientje yelled, "come downstairs to the air-raid shelter with Opoe and me."

"But the neighbors."

"Nobody's out in the street now. Come. You can't get killed now." Her voice cracked. "Annie."

"I'm coming as fast as I can."

Dientje half-carried me into the shelter.

"Opoe, are you here?"

"Ja, ja, where else? Where's that Johan? They wouldn't have taken the horse."

"Yes, they would've. But why isn't he back? I'm scared. Oh, my God, did you hear that? Johan," Dientje wailed.

"Keep your wits together. Annie, you scared?"

I made myself as small as possible. You know a bomb can hit you, don't you? Can kill you, too. After two years and seven months upstairs, it could be a bomb, not a murder camp. Ha, outside. You may never leave the shelter. Listen to that noise. Just listen. Who wants to be liberated if it means this? The way it was was all right. I didn't mind. No, I don't mean that. I did mind. I did.

"You here?" Johan came in. "Annie, too? Good."

"Why were you out in the street? Why didn't you come back sooner? You could've gotten killed, you. You're so smart." Was Dientje crying?

"It's mostly over now," Johan said in a toneless voice. "You should see what happened. A bomb hit the bakery. Killed the old mother and the young people. Another bomb hit the parsonage. It's in a shambles, but nobody was inside."

"Where were you, Johan?"

"On my stomach in a meadow. I saw it all. Boy, o boy, what a mess! They were Canadian airplanes."

"Why did they throw a bomb on the bakery?" Dientje asked.

"I don't know. A mistake, I guess."

"Some mistake. The parsonage was a mistake, too? Where's the minister."

"I saw him, Ma. He's okay. Let's go in the house. They're gone."

"I met the Hanninks," Johan said upstairs, "right after the bombing. You should've seen Mr. Hannink. He was trembling. He was. I said to'm, What's the matter? You're used to danger. What're you so afraid of? You know, he hardly answered me. He couldn't. His teeth were clattering. I'm not kidding. Boy, to be so scared. I didn't like it either, but I wasn't. . . ."

"Their house get hit, too? They're so close to the bakery." Dientje interrupted him.

"The windows broke. That's all."

"That's Sini by the kitchen door, Johan."

Johan looked out of the window. "You're right. Hey, you should've stayed home. Just because it's Saturday night doesn't mean you've got to be out."

"I had to come here. I've never milked so fast in my life."

"Did anything happen out your way?"

"Nothing like here. I was so afraid something had happened to you."

"Johan, there's somebody else at the door."

"That's Dini Hannink? I just saw her. What's up, Dini? Your father a little calmer?"

"The Canadians are coming tomorrow."

"Those planes again?" Opoe asked.

"No, soldiers. We'll be free around noon."

"How d'you know, Dini?"

"From somebody who knows. The planes cleared the way today. There shouldn't be any fighting tomorrow. Those few Germans that are still around will have left by then."

"I'll be damned," Johan said. "We'll be free."

"It sure would be nice to have a drop of coffee now," Opoe said, "the real stuff. Do Canadians or Americans, or whatever they are, drink coffee?"

"Sure, Opoe."

"Then Johan, you better ask for some. You speak what they do."

"I sure do. 'Coffee you have me,' I'll say. Sini, how's that for a dumb farmer?"

"Beautiful, Johan."

Why am I so calm, as if this is an ordinary evening? Aren't you glad? Yes, but I don't feel any different, not excited or anything. Maybe it's just as well, in case it doesn't happen. What am I going to do if it does happen? Go out? What if there's a German left? You know, there has to be only one. That would be enough. Just one. I did feel different. Uncomfortably I wriggled on my chair.

"Sini, you'll be here tomorrow, won't you?" Johan asked.

"Of course. I'm asking for the day off."

"Don't tell 'em yet who you are," Dientje warned.

"I'll be damned. Tomorrow."

Why tomorrow? After those bombs, it should be

today. Maybe there'll be more planes tomorrow. We can still get killed, just like those people in the bakery. My face felt hot, and sweaty.

"I won't be able to sleep all night," Opoe said. "Why bother to try."

"You've got to, Ma. Tomorrow you'll be busy."

"Ja, ja. With what?"

"Aren't you coming with us to watch the Canadians?"

"Me? No. I'm not starting now. Watching Canadians. Hendrik should know."

12

I GOT up and took my dress out of the closet. Off with you, pajamas. Yep, today I'd have to get dressed. Can you imagine going out in your pajamas, Annie? I started to laugh. Nope. What if they're not coming? I sat down on the bed. Then what? Quit it. Dini said they would. But it's the first of April, April Fools' Day.

"No, Opoe, I can't eat any breakfast." She was early, wanted to get all the work out of the way, too. Like me. I smoothed my dress.

"Eat just a little bit. You'll get so thin. And that's the worst thing that can happen to people."

"All right, Opoe." If it made her feel better, why not?

She sighed with relief.

"Sini, you're here already. What did they say?" Sini was early, too.

"Oh, nothing." She sat down in front of the mirror

as if she had never been away. "I'm so happy. Do I look good? Let me fix your hair. They're going to be here soon. Hello, Canadian soldiers, how nice to see you. I wonder what color uniforms they have. I hear Mr. Hannink downstairs. Wait a minute, Annie, I'll be right back."

I picked up the mirror. Bewilderedly I stared at myself. What a pale face. Bah! And hair that was half red and half black. Bah, bah! Sini's so excited. Aren't you? Yes, I am. Of course. I do look better when I smile. That's what I'll do outside. Hello everybody, you're looking at an ex-prisoner. Why was I a prisoner? I forget. I think because I'm Jewish. A long time? Boy, was it! Well, never mind. Today had better be the day though.

Sini came back with Opoe, who was wearing her Sunday apron.

"Mr. Hannink has already seen them," Sini said jubilantly.

"Where?"

"In Boekelo. They're on their way. They'll be in Usselo in half an hour or so. Come on."

"Where are we going?"

"Outside, of course. They're coming on the main road. Yes, you look fine. Do I? C'mon sister, hurry."

"Opoe, you come, too."

"No, no."

"But Opoe, this is such a special day. You must."

"Okay, because you want me to. I guess Hendrik wouldn't mind. I've been home a long time. Wait till I get my cap." She opened the bottom drawer of the

184

chest. "It never got right after that heavy book," she complained. "Boy, was I mad." With stiff fingers she tied the strings under her chin.

"What are you thinking about, Annie? Let's go."

Reluctantly I followed Sini down the stairs. I haven't been outside for so long that I don't even want to go. I'll wait for another day. But I can go near the window in the front room. I can stand right up against it, because we're free after all. And then when I see somebody, I won't duck. I'll stay, even raise my hand. Hello. How are you?

"Come, or I'll have to carry you," Johan said, "and I'm not kidding." I took Dientje's and Sini's hands. We left the kitchen, went along the side of the house, walked through the gate, and turned left. I looked back. The house was just as Johan had described it. Red brick with green trimmings.

Who is that? Somebody is looking at me. I want to go back before it's too late. Too late for what? I don't know, but I don't like to be stared at. I have a scarf on, so it can't be my hair. It must be my legs. Are they really that different from other people's? They must be. My face burned.

"Morning, Johan. What a day of all days. Right? Your mother looks good. You should take her out more often."

"Ja, Willem, but you know how they get when they're old."

"Ja, ja, I know. Having guests?"

"Yes. I'll tell you about 'em later. Now we're in a

hurry." Johan pushed me on. "Let's move a little faster, Annie, or we'll miss them."

Miss them? If we didn't see them, what would happen? Sure, we should hurry. I pushed my shoulders back a little bit. I wasn't going to miss them.

"I should've worn different wooden shoes," Opoe complained. "These hurt me."

"Look, that's where the bakery was."

"God-o-god-o-god, Johan, I wish I hadn't come. What's the matter with those Canadians?"

"Morning, Gerrit. Yes, we're on our way, too. You're right. I know. Yes, the girls are friends. I'll tell you about 'em later."

"Let's not stand near all those people, Johan."

"Stop it, woman. Let's stand on this rubble. That's where the parsonage was. No, Groothuis, they're not from Usselo. Later. And you especially listen carefully."

"Ja, ja, not for twenty-two years. No, this is special. I'm not going out again. You can't fool me. I know how old I am. Isn't it a shame about the parsonage? Such a nice man, the minister, too. And all those books. They must've burned. He had some really heavy ones, too. Fui-fui-fui, what this world isn't like!" Opoe wiped her eyes.

There were the Hanninks. They winked.

"Now he's brave again. You should've seen him yesterday."

"Annie, don't wave at the Hanninks. Better not. Later."

"Where will the soldiers come from?"

"That way. Can't be long now. Morning, Piet. Yes, those girls are friends. I'll explain later."

"Annie, your scarf's coming off. Fix it."

"Johan, I've got to sit down some place. Those wooden shoes don't fit."

There, there! They were coming, sitting in and on tanks, waving at everybody. Hello, too. I don't have to fix the scarf anymore. Hello.

Johan walked up to one of the tanks. "Have you cigarettes me? Hey, that fellow understands me. Look, he threw me a package."

"That Johan."

"Thanks. I wish this tank would pass a little bit faster, then I can ask the next fellow. Hey, you cigarettes me? Goddammit, that one must be a tight-fisted one. He did understand me. Son of a gun."

"Ask for coffee, Johan."

I looked around. Where had Sini gone? Oh, my God, she was climbing on a tank. Throwing her arms around a soldier's neck. Kissing him before she jumped down.

"God-o-god-o-god, that Sini. What's next!"

Hello. Tears on my face? But I'm not crying. I am. I'm crying. I am. So glad. Why did it take you soldiers so long? So awfully long. I'm not mad. Today? How could I be. Hello. I love you. Sounds funny, but I mean it. All of you. Hello, hello.

More and more farmers stood around Johan. They

looked from him to Sini and me. Who were the strangers he had brought? they kept asking. "Not that it's any of our business, but you know, you hate to keep guessing."

In a loud voice Johan answered. "They're Jewish girls we had in the house. Aw, it was nothing. No, I was never afraid. Never. Not even when we had those German soldiers. Ah, that was nothing. I'd do it again. Here, Ma? Boy, she's a tough one. Dientje, admit it. You weren't always cool. Hello, you cigarettes me? How d'you like my English, eh? This one taught me how to talk it. Thanks. What kind of stuff did that one throw me? Plum pudding. What's that?"

"They look like nice fellows, Johan."

"They are, Ma. Look at that Sini climbing on a tank again. Annie, get her, or she'll be off to the next town." He turned to the farmers again. "Yes, the Hanninks had 'em for a while. Couple of months. We had 'em for over two years. They're good girls. We didn't tell anybody about 'em. Don't be mad. It would've been too dangerous if we had told everybody in Usselo. I know you're special, but don't forget that I was responsible for them. No, I was never afraid. Not me. Hey, Groothuis, take a look at my girls.

"You aren't surprised? Hey, why not? Annie, I thought you'd never been near that window. Oh, I see. We had the light on upstairs an awful lot at night. You see, this town is just a dumb place. Sini's right. Just a minute. You cigarettes me?"

"Johan stop that begging. You cough enough."

"Leave me alone, woman. Ask 'em for some of those cans. That stuff looks good. Me cans, you say. Annie, how d'you feel?"

I just wave. Welcome!

"Let's go home. My feet bother me."

"All right, Ma. I guess we can't stand here all day. Good-bye Hanninks. See you."

"How do you girls feel?"

"Great, Mrs. Hannink."

To tell you the truth, I don't feel a thing. My hands just move up and down. Good-bye, soldiers, we have to go home.

Half a dozen farmers followed us back to the house. Inside I stood in the corner of the kitchen. Was I supposed to go upstairs now? Maybe so.

"Stay here, silly girl. You don't have to go upstairs anymore. You can all come in, Gerrit, Piet, Groothuis, everybody." Johan got chairs.

"Poor girls. Look at that little one. So pale. You can see she hasn't been outside for a long time." "Wasn't it hard? What did you do all day? You must be glad it's over." "We didn't like the war either. Where d'you come from." "Winterswijk? You have any father or mother?" "Well, maybe your father's still alive." "A sister, too? Older than you two?" "Yes, those Germans were bad. Really bad." "Haven't I seen you in the neighborhood lately, a couple of times a week?" "I said to myself, I wonder how that girl knows the Oostervelds. But you know, you don't want to be nosy." "So you worked there for a few months. How are they? They didn't grow up around here." "They're nice, though? Well, well, what a day this has been." They all left together, still talking.

Johan wiped his forehead. "Well, wife, put some of that food out that I got you today."

"This meat in the can," Opoe said, "is no good. It has no taste."

"But it's soft enough, Opoe."

"It sticks to my gums. I wonder how they make that stuff." Opoe picked up the empty can and turned it around in her hands. "Is this English?"

"Yes."

"English! Hendrik should know." She lifted her apron to wipe her eyes.

"Come sit on my lap," Dientje said to me. "Or don't you like me anymore now that you're free? You know, in a few days you're going back to Winterswijk."

"I'll go first and take a look," Johan said.

What would I do in Winterswijk? Go back to school? What grade? Nobody would remember me. Frits? Pooh. I went back to my own chair.

"It sure was nice having you," Opoe said.

"You talk, Ma, as if you'll never see them again. They'll come a lot, you'll see."

"I know, but it won't be the same."

"Will you miss me a little bit?" Dientje asked.

"Sure."

"You'll forget me, that big woman from Usselo."

"But Dientje, we won't. We couldn't."

"And that dumb farmer. You'll get so fancy."

"Stop it, Johan."

"I want you to come for my birthday every year," Opoe said, "for those few I've left."

"Okay, Opoe."

"Will you write sometimes?"

"Of course."

I straightened my legs under the table. They hurt. People had looked at them today. They will in Winterswijk, too. Would kids ignore me? Pretend I wasn't there. Or stop talking when I came close? Because they didn't want me to know what they were saying? Would they . . . ?

My lips felt dry. What a day! Who had said that? One of the farmers. He was right.

"Well," Johan yawned, "let's go to bed."

Opoe stood up first. "My poor bones. Fui-fui. Soon."

We kissed her. "Good night, Opoe. Sleep well."

She looked pleased, "I won't, but it's nice enough of you to want me to." Slowly she went upstairs. Johan and Dientje followed. Then Sini and I.

At the top of the stairs we stood still. Opoe was standing in the doorway uncoiling her brown braid. She stroked it. "I got this from my sister, too. Such fine stuff she had."

"Where do you want us to sleep, Dientje?" Sini asked.

"You can stay in the front room. Johan and I'll sleep in the back."

"Hey, woman, our bed used to be good enough for Annie. And Sini did fine on the floor. Eh?"

"Johan, the war's over."

"You know, I'm beginning to wish it wasn't. We used to have good times. Goddammit, now it's over."

"Johan, what'll the girls think?"

"They know me."

"And Hendrik used to be so soft-spoken."

"Well, good night." But nobody moved.

"You want something to eat before you go to sleep?"

"No, Opoe, we're full."

"Annie, I'm going to make you another dress so you'll have two when you go back to Winterswijk. I have another one of mine I can cut up. Nice little checks."

"C'mon, woman. It's late."

"Maybe we can get you some wooden shoes now, too." Dientje's face was red.

"You're not leaving tomorrow, are you? To Winterswijk? Johan, not tomorrow?" Opoe asked.

"No, I think I'll wait a couple of days till the roads are safe."

"Maybe a week, Johan." Opoe's voice was trembling.

"Now, let's go, woman. I've got to get up early. Want to help me with the cows, Sini?"

"Sure."

"Now that she can be useful she's going away."

"Johan, she shouldn't have to work here."

"But, Ma, she likes to."

"Ja, ja, I don't understand. We just do it."

"Doesn't she have to tell the farmer that she won't be back, Johan?"

"I'll go with her tomorrow. I'd like to see his face. Now, c'mon."

"Johan, the girls can't come with you when you go to Winterswijk. You've got to see for yourself first."

"I know, Ma."

"Well, good night, then," Dientje said awkwardly, "I guess there's nothing we can do." She and Johan went into the back room.

"Back to Winterswijk," Opoe said with tears in her eyes. "What's next?"

Quietly Sini and I slipped into the front room. The shade was up.

Boldly I passed the safe side of the bed. Another step and I was in front of the window. I pushed my nose against it. There was the street and the Groothuises' house.

Somebody on a bicycle passed. I ducked.

"What are you doing?"

That's right, you don't have to anymore, Annie. The war is over. You'll get used to it. I pulled the shade down and got into bed.

"Good night, Sini."

"Good night, little sister."

Postscript

A week went by, and Johan still had not gone to Winterswijk. "Tomorrow," he kept saying. When tomorrow came, nobody reminded him of it. Then Rachel arrived in Usselo, on foot, since no buses were running and no one had tires left on their bikes.

"It can be done in one day," she said, "if you're as anxious as I was to get here."

It was nice to be with her until she mentioned that she had come to take us back to Winterswijk.

"I can't go yet," Sini said. "I'm dating this boy, and I'm just getting to know him."

"And I'm not leaving either," I said. "I'm just getting used to being able to go outside here." Defiantly I looked around the kitchen. Nobody would make me go.

So Rachel went to Winterswijk by herself, to clean the house.

It was almost a month later before Sini and I left Usselo, in her boyfriend's rusty car. The few clothes we had were wrapped in old newspapers, the no-good-kind, the ones with all the lies. In my pocket was the money Mother had given me the last time I saw her.

Opoe stood in the doorway. She cried. "You're closer to me than my own family. What am I going to do now?"

The boyfriend started up the car.

Johan blew his nose. "Damn."

"Don't forget us," Dientje called out.

Slowly we drove away, waving.

Father was in Winterswijk, too. Our life there started again.

After a while both Rachel and Sini left. So did I eventually, to come to America. In my trunk was the lace cap Opoe had given me when I had gone to say goodbye. "Put it on top of your clothes, not underneath," she told me, "so it won't happen again. You remember—that heavy book?"

Four years ago I took my two children to Usselo.

"You Holland talk?" Johan asked them.

They shook their heads. No.

The two of them sat on Dientje's lap, staring at Opoe.

"You really should've gotten false teeth, Opoe," I said. "All these years you've been miserable because you didn't."

"Nonsense," she said, "I got used to it. And now it doesn't make any sense. Soon."

She was ninety-two then.

I took my girls upstairs to the front room. Johan had left the hiding place intact.

"That's the place Mommy used to crawl into," I said.

"See whether you can do it now," they asked me.

Obediently I went over to the closet and got on the floor.

That's as far as I got.

"Look, she's crying," my girls said.

ABOUT THE AUTHOR

Johanna Reiss did not set out to write a book about her experiences during the Second World War; she simply wanted to record them for her two daughters. "I didn't think it would take me more than a week!" she says. "Not until I started to write did I find out how much I remembered, things I had never talked about with anyone because they were too painful."

THE UPSTAIRS ROOM has received many honors and awards; it was selected as a Newbery Honor Book, an American Library Association Notable Children's Book, and a Jane Addams Peace Association Honor Book. It also won the Jewish Book Council Juvenile Book Award and the Buxtehuder Bulle, a prestigious German children's book award.

The author continues the story begun in THE UPSTAIRS ROOM with a sequel, entitled THE JOURNEY BACK, in which Annie de Leeuw and her sister Sini rejoin their father and older sister and struggle to reclaim their former life.

Johanna Reiss was born and brought up in Holland. After she graduated from college, she taught elementary school for several years before coming to the United States. She now lives in New York City.